THE LIFE AND TIMES
OF ROBERT G. FOWLER

A Pictorial History

MARIA SCHELL BURDEN

BORDEN PUBLISHING COMPANY
LOS ANGELES, CALIFORNIA
1999

THE LIFE AND TIMES OF ROBERT G. FOWLER
A Pictorial History

COVER DESIGN BY MARCI BISHOP
SCANNING BY TERRY WALKER

BORDEN PUBLISHING COMPANY
2623 SAN FERNANDO ROAD
LOS ANGELES, CALIFORNIA 90065

PRINTED IN THE U.S.A.

ISBN 0-87505-369-6

＆

For Kellen and Sydney,
my faithful companions at libraries,
aviation events and museums when they would rather
have been skating or at the movies.

＆

TABLE OF CONTENTS

ACKNOWLEDGEMENTS

The development of this book has been possible because of the contributions of many people. My publisher Joe Campbell dedicated more than two years of intensive research and travel to uncover the tremendous volume of information available in the most obscure locations.

We gratefully acknowledge the generous contributions of the late Gloria DeVargas Bush and her family, who made accessible to us Robert G. Fowler's extensive collection of memorabilia and photographs of their "Daddy Bob."

The people of Colfax (especially Gertrude Paul and Joan Meyers), Auburn and Nevada City, California have provided invaluable information and support for this project. They have our sincere gratitude for the many photographs and personal stories of Bob Fowler's adventures in their towns. As a result of this book, a bronze plaque now marks the site in Colfax where Bob and his crew painstakingly restored the Wright after his crash at Alta and prepared it for a flight across the Sierras.

We would like to thank Robert Berryessa, Ed and Charlene Fontana, Pat Jones, Ray Wagner, Barbara Keeney, J.L. Johnson Jr., Jean Strickland, Trish Page, Janet Peters, Leonard McKay, Dawne Dewey, Cynthia Coan, Mark Cave, Patricia Baldwin Snar, Karen Bullard, Jean Wallace, David Montgomery, John Kensit, Bill Sagar, Doris Thomas, John P. Ingle, Jr., Nancy Martin and James S. Ricklefs, whose assistance in research in their particular areas was of inestimable importance.

Special thanks is owed to the following institutions for the generous contributions of their staff of time and diligence in research: The Gilroy Historical Museum, Searls Historical Library, Dunbar Library at Wright State University, State Library of Louisiana, Historic New Orleans Collection of the Kemper and Leila Williams Foundation, Banning Public Library, Biloxi Public Library, Mobile Public Library, Beaumont Public Library, Tyrell Historical Library and San Jose Public Library.

I am grateful to my dear mother, Patricia Schell of Sacramento, who spent a great deal of time researching local newspapers for facts about the first few days of Fowler's transcontinental journey. She helped bring Fowler's adventures to life and has always encouraged me to aim high. And thanks to Kent who has always believed that I could achieve anything.

Robert G. Fowler in 1911 at the controls of his new Wright biplane, the "Cole Flyer." This picture was taken a few days before the start of his transcontinental flight. Courtesy San Diego Aerospace Museum.

INTRODUCTION

❦

Few people alive today can comprehend what it meant to live in America in the early 1900s. Encroaching urbanization, the settlement of the American west, and the rapid development of new technologies made the sky the limit of man's pioneering efforts. Those who dared to attempt its conquest were considered heroes, if not a little crazy. Man's earliest attempts at flight are well documented, and a great debt is owed those who risked their lives in the development of the first commercially available aircraft.

Hundreds of books and thousands of articles have been published on the history of American aviation and its intrepid pioneers. From balloonist Thaddeus Lowe and his Civil War Balloon Corps to Orville and Wilbur Wright to Charles Lindbergh and Amelia Earhart, accounts of death-defying flights, record-setting journeys and ticker-tape parades swell our collective memory and dominate our vision of a glamorous quest for fame and fortune in the skies. Americans know and love these intrepid heroes. But one is missing.

One pioneer's ground-breaking aviation experiments and fearless endeavors in the competitive realm of early flight have been largely unrecounted. His endless optimism and drive to complete the task at hand, coupled with his notable accomplishments seem at odds with his relative obscurity to date. A skilled and resourceful mechanic, he was an intuitive aviator who, unlike many of his contemporaries, lived to old age and witnessed the beginnings of the era of jet airplanes and even space exploration. Let us introduce you to Robert G. Fowler.

We cannot hope to convey to you through a series of historic photographs alone all that made Robert G. Fowler who he was. Aviation enthusiasts deserve to know Bob Fowler's remarkable story.

The author, when possible, has included detailed reports of salient events and stories of local residents or newspaper writers who witnessed Fowler's exploits and/or disasters. But the real story here is in the pictures. Robert G. Fowler comes to life for us on these pages, and most clearly in these photographs.

What cannot be missed as one studies this group of rare photographs, many from Fowler's private collection, and numerous private collections throughout the United States and Panama, is that Fowler was at home at the controls of an aeroplane.

His deep understanding of mechanics and aerodynamics gave him the ability to grasp any problem and create a solution. But it was his spirit that took him to great heights. Optimism was Fowler's greatest asset. He felt that all things were possible and when he set his mind to accomplish a task, nothing but completion was acceptable. He would keep trying until he found the right solution.

This book is a combination of photographs, some of which tell their own story, and rather detailed accounts of his most remarkable achievements. While the quality of some photographs may be less than perfect, we felt that their inclusion was necessary to fully illustrate the Robert G. Fowler story.

❦

Chapter One

FROM DIRT TRACKS TO BLUE SKIES

ॐ

Robert Grant Thomas Fowler was born August 10, 1883 in San Francisco, California. He was the only child of Thomas James and Mary Francis (Ashworth) Fowler. His father was a rancher, hotel manager and garage owner. Robert spent much of his childhood as others did in those days--playing with friends, attending public schools and helping to run the family business in Gilroy.

After completing his education in 1901 at the age of eighteen, his parents gave him his first automobile, the first single cylinder Oldsmobile ever purchased in California. He traveled during the remainder of that year, and became a sales agent for Oldsmobile autos on the west coast. He was known by this time as a skilled mechanic and driver who had set records racing cars between San Francisco and Los Angeles. His fourteen-hour time stood as the record for several years.

In 1903, the world followed the progress of the Wright brothers and their experiments with heavier-than-air flight. When they met with success in December of that year at Kitty Hawk, North Carolina, Robert Fowler devoured the details of the flight reported in such journals as *Scientific American*. Also that year he raced a Franklin car with a four cylinder air cooler and won against the legendary race car driver Barney Oldfield. His speeds during the ten mile race at Ingleside Race Track topped one mile per minute.

In the early days of automobiles, individuals who could afford a car often hired drivers (chauffeurs), who also served as mechanics to operate the cantankerous motors and maintain the cars. In 1906 he began a European tour, employed as a chauffeur for the Diamonds, a wealthy San Francisco family. The earthquake and fire of 1906 forced their temporary return to California. He experienced numerous aftershocks to the great quake which he described in letters to his family in Gilroy. He described difficult driving conditions in the city, and the need to wear goggles at all times because of the brick and lime dust in the air which could cause a driver to "lose one's eyesight at any time."

During 1907, in the continuation of his European tour of eight countries, Fowler became interested in aviation in Paris, where he saw a dirigible fly overhead during the Bastille Day celebration. He also inspected the manufacturing plants of various European automobiles.

He became an expert on engines, propulsion and speed working with early automobiles like Oldsmobile, Packard, Cadillac, Pope-Toledo, Mercedes, Chalmers, Franklin, and Royal, among others.

Between 1908 and 1910 he developed various automobile garages and dealerships in the San Francisco area. He was again exposed to aviation at the Dominguez Air Meet in Los Angeles, California. This time, Robert Fowler's sights shifted irrevocably from dirt tracks to blue skies.

Robert's boyhood home in Gilroy, California. His family managed the Holloway Hotel on the Live Oak Ranch. Years later the building became The Oaks Apartments and the structure was moved several blocks away where it still stands.

*Frances "Faye" Fowler,
Robert's mother*

*Thomas James Fowler,
Robert's father*

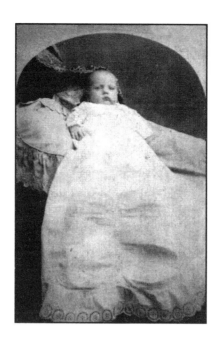

Robert Fowler as a baby and as a toddler.

"Robbie" at about six years of age

Gilroy High School Track and Field team photograph, probably 1899 or 1900. Bob Fowler is third from left in the back row, wearing the hat.

Faye Fowler as a young woman.

This photo was probably taken during his college days in San Francisco. Fowler attended Heald College in 1901, studying engineering, wireless, and Spanish. In 1902 he attended the University of California. But engines and high speeds held more intrigue...and more immediate thrills.

Bob's love of automobiles became central to his life shortly after high school graduation in 1901, when his parents bought him his first car, an Oldsmobile. His social scene during these years revolved almost exclusively around automobiles, racing and breaking records. Fowler became known as "the fastest man on wheels," and one of the best-known automobile racers in the west. He set numerous records including the world's record speed for a ten mile race in 1905 at the Del Monte Speedway in a four cylinder Pope-Toledo car. His fourteen hour time from Los Angeles to San Francisco remained the record for several years.

By 1910, Fowler had begun to feel that he had accomplished all he could in the world of automobile racing. To his mother's dismay, his curiosity turned skyward. Fellow racers Rex Younge and Louis DeMars were experimenting with an airplane they had recently purchased. Courtesy San Jose Mercury News.

CHAPTER TWO

ACROSS THE CONTINENT

❦

It is difficult to say exactly when Robert Fowler first became enamored of aviation. In his personal notes he states simply that during the year 1910 he "became interested in aeroplanes," and decided to "begin experimentation in this line..."

He read stories in *Scientific American* magazine of the earliest aviation accomplishments of Orville and Wilbur Wright and Glenn Curtiss in their glorified box kites made of bamboo, cotton cloth and bycicle tape. He was captivated when two friends, Louis DeMars, a fellow auto racer, and Rex Younge, a motorcycle racer, bought an aeroplane and invited Bob along to try it out in a northern California field.

The plane was under-powered and could only bounce along the ground at dizzying speeds of forty miles per hour in a straight line, and make brief hops into the air. Mid-air turns could not be practiced due to insufficient altitude. Nonetheless, young Bob Fowler was intoxicated with the notion of flight. Ready to demonstrate, DeMars assured Fowler that he would show him the basics of flying. So, with confidence DeMars climbed behind the controls.

Rex spun the single propeller and let go. DeMars and the plane surged forward. Bob watched with the fascination of a novice, observing the plane and DeMars racing and bouncing along the ground, without immediate knowledge that something was terribly wrong. Just then, Younge started jumping up and down, shouting "The controls! The controls!" The plane was going forty miles per hour when Bob observed DeMars, who now understood the problem, climbing out the rear of the moving aircraft.

A sturdy fence at the end of the field was rapidly approaching. Unable to do anything to help, Fowler and Younge watched and waited for the crack-up. DeMars was now hanging on for dear life to the rear of the frame, dragging his feet, attempting to stop the plane from reaching the fence. It came soon enough. The plane slammed into the fence, with DeMars still clinging to the frame. DeMars was uninjured, but he'd dragged his feet and pulled so hard trying to slow down the plane that he'd torn off the soles of his shoes.

"What happened?" asked Fowler as he and Younge arrived breathlessly at the wreck. DeMars shot a look at Younge, who sheepishly explained that the night before, he had carefully lashed the controls for safety, and forgotten to untie them that morning.The amateur trio examined the wreck. The rudder and controls, which before the flight had projected ten feet out in front of the aircraft, were now wedged back under the wings. Bob could scarcely believe that his first chance to fly was gone in a twisted heap right before his eyes.

Younge and DeMars determined that the motor and wings were undamaged. Fowler helped them remove the rudder, steering line and controls, and together the men took to the machine with a sledge hammer and some bicycle tape. They had her in flying shape within a few hours. Bob would finally get his chance at the controls the next day, and the experience would change him forever. Unaccustomed to being a novice at things mechanical, he felt a rush of adrenalin as DeMars reviewed the basics for the last time. "She's already cracked up once, Fowler, so you can't do any real harm." His head filled with the task at hand, Bob forced a thin smile at DeMars.

Far more confident in Fowler's ability than Fowler himself, DeMars pulled the single propeller through, and swung it. The motor thundered and the aircraft surged forward as DeMars let go. In seconds Bob was racing down the field at forty miles per hour with the dreaded fence approaching quickly. He pulled on the elevator lever and nothing happened--or so he thought. What had he done wrong? What had he forgotten? He looked down and realized that he was about ten feet off the ground. A rush of exhilaration saturated his senses.

He was flying! He might as well have been five hundred feet up, so great was his excitement. He skimmed the length of the field with a grin on his face. He set the battered aeroplane down at the end of the field, and vowed that he would find a way to make his living at flying.

Newspaper magnate William Randolph Hearst, after taking his first thrilling aeroplane ride with aviator Louis Paulhan, announced that he would pay $50,000 to the first aviator to fly from one U.S. coast to the other in thirty days or less, using just one aeroplane. The Hearst prize, calculated to create additional excitement for the new field of aviation, would also sell Hearst newspapers, which would liberally cover the race from beginning to end. A one-year time limit was imposed, the purse to be withdrawn after October 10, 1911. After initial excitement over the generous prize subsided, few aviators of the day showed any real intention of entering the race.

Most involved in aviation at the time, including Orville and Wilbur Wright, felt that such a lengthy journey would exceed the limits of aircraft technology at the time, between power limitations and durability of aircraft structure itself. Short exhibition flights were the ideal use for 1910-1911 era aeroplanes. The Wrights felt that long-distance flights should be put off until advances could be made in the current designs.

During 1910 after a record-setting automobile race from Los Angeles to San Francisco, Bob returned to southern California to attend the 1910 Dominguez Air Meet in January. Eugene Ely, a former racing partner of Bob's was the leading pilot for the Curtiss Exhibition Team. Ely introduced Bob Fowler to Glenn Curtiss, recounting tales of races won, records broken and mechanical challenges overcome.

Racing commitments would consume most of that year, but now the aviation bug had bitten hard, and was quickly burrowing under the skin of Bob Fowler. He returned to southern California in December of 1910 to attend the Los Angeles Air Carnival. He was convinced that even with his limited flying experience, he could show Glenn Curtiss what he had if he could just get a tryout. Curtiss, who had seen several of his exhibition pilots hospitalized that day after aerial mishaps, was in desperate need of a pilot for his remaining undamaged aeroplanes.

With Gene Ely's glowing endorsement of his former racing partner still in mind, Curtiss agreed to give Bob Fowler a tryout for the exhibition team. But Bob soon learned that he would be sharing the stage with another newcomer, Lincoln Beachey, who would get the first tryout.

Beachey, at 23 years old, had already made a name for himself as a dirigible pilot and had been on the Curtiss payroll for a short time as a mechanician. In limited training by Curtiss himself, Beachey had demonstrated a patent lack of instinct in making turns and landings, and had a tendency toward minor wrecks. As a pilot, Beachey was hard on a team's aircraft inventory and so had remained employed only as a mechanician in the Curtiss camp.

But on this day, Glenn Curtiss had a unique problem-- an aeroplane at an aviation meet with no one to fly it. He hesitated to take the controls himself. As president of the company, he had other responsibilities.

Curtiss had at least seen Beachey fly. This new guy Fowler was a complete unknown. Did he really have the experience he claimed to have? Curtiss flipped a mental coin and decided to give Beachey the first try-out. Beachey wrecked twice making dangerous turns, and Curtiss decided that he could not risk any more of his aeroplanes on novice pilots. Fowler left Curtiss and Beachey behind for the moment and returned to northern California without taking the controls even once.

Bob knew that his call to aviation could not go unanswered, but he must return to what he knew best and wait for an opportunity. It would come from an unlikely source-- auto racing. Bob Fowler was hired in 1911 to promote the latest automobile model of the Indianapolis, Indiana-based Cole Motor Company. The car was dubbed "The Cole Flyer." The significance of the name was not lost on Bob Fowler. True to his nature, he began to research and plan a strategy that he hoped would bring his dreams of flight to fruition.

He convinced company President J.J. Cole that the most exciting way to promote the Cole Flyer was from coast to coast, with Fowler himself competing in the Hearst transcontinental air race. Cole thought it was a splendid idea, and immediately advanced $7,500 toward the purchase of the most reliable aircraft of it's time. Bob's recommendation was the Wright Model B to be dubbed the "Cole Flyer."

With the wad from Cole in his pocket, he left for Simms Station, Dayton, Ohio to enroll in the Wright Company School of Aviation. He would be required to pass a qualification test for the Hearst race, and could take care of all details in one spot. There were numerous aviation schools for aspiring birdmen to choose from even in the infancy of aviation. The Wright's philosophy was markedly different than most. Students were extensively trained on the ground and always flew side-by-side with an instructor who held duplicate controls in the event of a student error. In the company's promotional literature the

Fowler's new Model B, soon to be named "Cole Flyer" being inspected prior to first flight at Huffman Prairie. At front of aeroplane, Bob Fowler at right, facing camera. Orville Wright is at left wearing the straw hat. Note men positioned behind the machine ready to spin the propellers for take off. Orville Wright advised Bob to cross the mountains via the southern route, fearing that the greater elevations (a minimum of 7,000 feet) in the Sierras might prove to be insurmountable. Courtesy Wright State University Photographic Archives.

school's policies were plainly stated: " the pupil is not held responsible for breakage of machines." At the rates they were charging, $250.00, "they could afford to fix a few aeroplanes," thought Fowler.

He arrived near the end of July, 1911 to receive instruction from the nation's pioneer fliers, and oversee production of his very own Wright Model B. As a seasoned mechanic, he knew the importance of familiarizing oneself with every aspect of a machine. He intended to be the most knowlegeable member of his mechanical crew, able to fix any problem for himself in the event that his crew was unable to reach him. After just a few hours of flight instruction under A.L.

(Al) Welsh, the Wright's most trusted pilot, Fowler made his first solo flight. Welsh declared that Bob Fowler was a fine pilot--the best airman he had ever taught. A swooping figure eight in the air qualified Bob as the first official entrant in the Hearst race. He was awarded Hydroaeroplane licence number 36.

On August 31, 1911 Bob filed his intention with the Hearst newspaper *The New York American* as the first official entrant in the transcontinental air race. Orville Wright, who had become fond of Bob, spent a great deal of time with him as he plotted his transcontinental course and discussed his plans with anyone who would listen. Orville tried more than once to convince Bob to leave from Los Angeles instead of San Francisco. The extreme elevations in the Sierra Nevada Range might be too much for the Wright and its small engine, even with a naturally skilled pilot like Fowler.

Bob would never forget a closed-door meeting in the upstairs office of the Wright Cycle Company at 1127 West Third Street in Dayton, Ohio. The brothers "really gave me a talking to about trying to fly across the continent," he would later say. Their strenuous attempt at talking their talented student out of the coast to coast flight even included an admission that their engine was quite unreliable in flights longer that one hour.

Bob argued that he was an experienced mechanic and could fix any problem without help from a crew. When it became

Bob at the controls of the Cole Flyer. Standing by are J.J. Cole and C. Fred Grundy of the Cole Motor Company, which later became part of Cadillac. Courtesy San Jose Mercury News.

obvious that their friend would not be talked out of it, they asked how they could help. Fowler picked their brains for several days, trouble-shooting various problems and making plans. Orville favored a southern route through the desert with its lower elevations.

Fowler asserted that the high elevations in the Sierras would force him to fly higher, thus affording him extra time to locate an emergency landing site and volplane to it in the event of an engine failure. Bob was determined to leave from his hometown of San Francisco, and it seemed that nothing would sway him.

Flight training was not the only aspect of planning that Fowler concentrated upon. He constructed a complex system to navigate the continent and maintain contact with his crew along the way. The only sure east-to-west guideline available was the railroad tracks, which Fowler now referred to as his "iron compass." Besides providing a visual guide, the

ATWOOD, RODGERS, FOWLER AND STONE FORMALLY JOIN LISTS FOR THE WORLD'S GREATEST AIR RACE

Three Ready to Start at Pacific Coast and One From Atlantic; Special Trains and Armies of Autos to Follow Aviators; Several European Entrants Are Expected.

railroad provided the additional advantage of having a crew and spare parts on the rails in the event of a forced landing. Accordingly, he made arrangements for a special train car which would follow his course. The Cole Motor Company would arrange for fuel, water and spare parts to be available at all times aboard the train, as well as at Fowler's scheduled stops. His mechanicians would also be present aboard the train.

His mother, Faye Fowler would be along for the ride, bringing with her the well-known boxing trainer Tim McGrath. Charged with monitoring Fowler's physical health at all times during the transcontinental journey, McGrath would order the aviator proper meals, set his sleep schedule, and control his exposure to crowds.

Meanwhile, the time limit for the Hearst prize was rapidly approaching. A start had to be made by the early part of September in order for the flight to be completed by the October 10 expiration date. Fowler calculated that he would need twenty flying days to complete the coast-to-coast journey, and would allow an additional ten days for rest, repairs and inclement weather. With that in mind, and the wind at his back, Fowler predicted it was an achievable goal.

The transcontinental air race was no small challenge. The sort of determination required to continue onward day after day against all kinds of adversity was not to be taken lightly. Thrill-seekers without any staying power would be quickly discouraged by such an undertaking. Fowler knew this better than any of his competitors. It would not be a comfortable journey. With freezing temperatures at high elevations, coupled with exposure to the wind, it would be a physical test as well as a mental one.

Long races were nothing new to Bob. His days behind the wheel of an automobile in long distance events would serve him well, but the particular challenges of an aviation race were still unknowns. Balancing the logical timeline of the trip with the grand ideas of a promoter proved to be one of the most difficult challenges of all.

As Fowler quietly worked behind the scenes, the number of entrants in the race grew, and soon twelve competitors had declared their intentions. To Fowler, the race and its successful completion was all. But his backers, of course, had their own agenda. As a commercial enterprise, the flight must achieve certain goals outside the arena of the Hearst prize, and of course sell cars in the bargain.

As excitement grew about the transcontinental race, cities began vying for the opportunity to host the beginning or end of the race. Local business associations collected purses, some rather impressive sums, to induce the pilots to make their start or finish there. In Fowler's home state of California, Los Angeles and San Francisco were the cities approved by the Hearst Rules Committee for start or finish.

Fowler had on his plate a mind-boggling list of arrangements and preparations to be made prior to the start of his journey. Meanwhile, Cal Rodgers, his principal competitor in the race, was planning a start from New York any day, and the pressure was on to be the first aviator officially underway.

After seeing to the safe delivery of his aircraft from the railroad express car a few weeks earlier, Bob had spent several days studying maps and railroad routes to plot his most favorable course through the Sierra Nevada Mountains - his most formidable obstacle in the race. Ever pragmatic, Fowler knew that careful planning could spell the difference between success and failure, perhaps even life and death.

He boarded an eastbound Southern Pacific freight train and traveled the Sierras between Colfax, California and Reno, Nevada. From an observation platform aboard the train, he noted possible forced landing sites and memorized the lay of the land and the elevations of key mountains.

The Cole Motor Company had appointed C. Fred Grundy, a Cole sales agent from Los Angeles as Fowler's manager for the cross-country journey. Grundy and Fowler often disagreed on details relating to the race. Fowler was naturally shy and not one to promote himself or brag about his accomplishments. Grundy's grandstanding on the aviator's behalf (part of his job as manager) made Fowler patently uncomfortable. Bob just wanted to get underway in the simplest, most timely fashion possible. Grundy, however, was determined that Fowler would start from whichever west coast city was willing to put up the largest financial incentive to that end. Fowler had made clear his preference for a start from San Francisco. A struggle for control ensued. Grundy initiated a series of communications to the cities of Los Angeles, San Francisco, Oakland, Pasadena, and others. He also contacted the official Hearst timekeepers in San Francisco, C.C. Moore and James Rolph Jr., who was also a candidate for mayor.

In the days leading up to the official departure date, Bay area newspapers scrambled to keep up with the latest location

Fowler prepares the Cole Flyer for her maiden flight at San Francisco's Golden Gate Park on September 11, 1911.

for the transcontinental take off. On Saturday, September 9, the *Oakland Tribune* complained that the aviation editor had to be summoned several times over the weekend to approve changes in copy that would more accurately report the Fowler party's latest take off date and location.

Grundy, a Los Angeles resident, thought that the city to the south would be most suitable. Fowler's initial plans had called for a start from San Francisco's Golden Gate Park on Sunday, September 10 at 10:00 a.m. When Grundy learned that a $10,000 purse awaited the aviator who would begin from Los Angeles, he began anew his campaign to convince Fowler to head south. In the end, Fowler won out.

San Francisco's Golden Gate Park was a blizzard of activity on Monday, September 11, 1911. Ten thousand spectators, roped-off from Fowler and his Wright biplane, pointed and shouted among themselves. The flimsy, kite-like appearance of the Cole Flyer only amplified skepticism that the aviator would reach his goal. For most, it was their first look at a flying machine. For all, it was a chance to witness the opening of a chapter in history.

The difficulties of the past few days began to melt away as the young aviator observed that the moment was finally here--he would actually begin the journey he had been seeking. It would be a test of man and machine as one to conquer the skies. A smooth start had seemed all but impossible until now. The press, eager for a quote, hovered nearby as Fowler checked and re-checked his machine. Mechanics Ralph Newcomb, Frank Murray and Adolf Sutro, in the first of many preflight performances, busily oiled and adjusted the engine of the Wright.

Onlookers studied Fowler's face for signs of trepidation, but found none. If Fowler was nervous, he wasn't showing it. A preliminary ten minute flight had confirmed his confidence that the machine was in perfect condition.

With goggles perched upon his sun-burned head, he eyed the hills ringing San Francisco, reminding himself that they were mere bumps compared to what he would face in the following days. The crowd was a formidable distraction, but Fowler's mind was on the biplane. So focused was his attention as he passed close to the ropes, that a young woman took him by surprise as she threw her arms around his neck and kissed him soundly. At that moment, another woman pinned to the lapel of his leather coat a badge proclaiming "Votes for Women." Thus read Tuesday's headline in the New York Times:

"START FROM SAN FRANCISCO
Fowler Hopeful of Success-He Wears a Sufragette Badge."

Fowler blushed deeply and moved quickly into the midst of his mechanical team completing their preparation of the Wright. Inside the ropes, San Francisco city officials and representatives of the army and navy circulated about the aviator and his machine. At 1:00 p.m. candidate for San Francisco Mayor James Rolph Jr. began the dedication ceremony, wielding a bottle of Pacific Ocean water to officially name the plane "Cole Flyer."

"May the tranquil influences of the placid waters of our Pacific, with which I have the honor to christen thee today 'Cole Flyer' be with you in your flight across the continent, and may you enable your daring aviator, guide and helmsman, to crown his efforts with success, is our parting Godspeed to you." He splashed a liberal amount of ocean water on the "Cole Flyer" and the crowd roared.

Fowler wings away from Golden Gate Park heading northeast.
Courtesy San Jose Mercury News.

"Thank you, Mr. Rolph," was Fowler's response when it was finally quiet again. "Your fight is nearly won, and mine is just beginning." Rolph would indeed go on to be elected Mayor of San Francisco.

As the ceremony was ending, Lieutenant Julius L. Dodge, who had just arrived at Golden Gate Park, rushed to Fowler and handed him an envelope. An aide to Brigadier General Daniel Brush, commander of the Department of California, Dodge delivered a written message to Major General Frederick D. Grant, commander of the Department of the East headquartered at Governor's Island, New York. It seemed that Fowler was to hand-deliver the message from Grant when he landed. He tucked the letter into his breast pocket.

With afternoon advancing, Fowler was eager to get underway. He kissed his mother, who blinked back tears and smiled proudly as she clasped both his hands. He shook hands with his father, then pulled on his leather gloves. He checked to be sure that the wheels were safely blocked. With the sufragette badge still pinned to his lapel, he climbed into the seat of the biplane and signaled for Sutro and Newcomb to swing the propellers.

The engine roared to life, forcing the wheels to surge against the blocks. The Cole Flyer seemed as ready as Fowler to take to the air. The aviator signaled his crew to remove the blocks, and the aircraft jumped forward, cruising along the grassy infield. Over the roaring engine, Fowler could not hear the crowd, but open mouths, waving hats and handkerchiefs told him he was being given the send-off of a hero. He grinned and gripped the controls more tightly, lifting the Wright into the air. He made a wide circle, the aviator's wave, over Golden Gate Park then headed north. Turning east he headed across San Francisco Bay and over the Oakland shore, leaving San Francisco behind.

Fowler's first afternoon at the controls of the Wright was a learning experience. His instincts as an automobile racer served him well at the controls of an aeroplane, but there were drastic differences between aviation and auto racing.

The crisp, salty coastal air gradually gave way to warmer inland breezes. He kept the Wright at an altitude of 800 feet, his eyes never ceasing to scan the earth below for a suitable landing site, just in case. Marking his path were the tracks of the Southern Pacific Railroad, which would also carry the special cars with his mother, his mechanical team and spare parts for the Wright. After about ninety minutes, the state capitol of Sacramento edged into view. Seated at the heart of the fertile central valley, the city was the halfway mark through his home state.

Fowler's visit created a unique opportunity for one of Sacramento's less distinguished residents. "Kid Nash," a petty thief serving a six month sentence in the Sacramento County Jail took advantage of the chief jailer's interest in Fowler's flight to take an unscheduled furlough. A regular at the jail, the "Kid" was working as an assistant cook when the jailers informed him that Fowler was about to fly over the city. Feigning interest, Nash ran to the window to look out as the jailers climbed the ladder to the roof. Nash took the elevator down and easily departed the building. A search was made, but Nash was not found. The following day a headline in the *Sacramento Union* declared: " Prisoner Escapes from Rubbernecks--Officer on Roof, 'Kid Nash' Aviates in Elevator."

Fowler surveyed the town, made a wide circle around the capitol building, then headed for the race track at the Agricultural Park on the outskirts. As the drone of the Wright's engine heralded Fowler's arrival, Sacramento residents shaded their eyes, looking skyward to follow his path to the open field where he would land. The plane rolled to a stop, and Fowler asked the first person to approach the Wright "What time is it?" Without waiting for an answer, he pulled out his own pocket watch, and declared "It's 3:28," as a *Sacramento Union* photographer snapped his photo. A car was sent for him, and the excited driver informed him that he was to be the guest of California's Governor Hiram W. Johnson at a luncheon across town.

At the Hotel Land, Fowler signed the register "R.G. Fowler, by air from San Francisco." Good wishes were piled on by all who met him, and his reply to each, whether a state legislator or a shoeshine boy, was a quiet and courteous "Thank you very much."

Although Faye Fowler and the crew had been due in Sacramento aboard the "Fowler Special" shortly after his arrival, they remained unaccounted for. A phone call was made to San Francisco and Fowler learned that there had been a delay in the special's departure. His entourage, he was informed, would not arrive in Sacramento until after 6:00 p.m. Fowler knew that he had to reach the foothills of the Sierra Nevadas by nightfall if he hoped to make his planned flight over the mountain range the next day. He made the decision to fly ahead. "I am not going to worry about the Special now," he said while eating lunch, "I'm going on with the flying and let the Special take care of itself. I'll get along all right."

Thomas Fowler, Bob's father, who owned a mechanical garage in the town of Gilroy, California, monitored his son's progress from a telegraph office in San Jose. Between bulletins as Bob reached landmarks along the way, his father proudly shared with reporters stories of his son's accomplishments. A holiday atmosphere prevailed in Gilroy, where many businesses closed for the day to keep tabs on the progress of their hometown hero.

Fowler stayed his first night at the Freeman Hotel in Auburn.

Back at the race track in Sacramento's Agricultural Park, Fowler purchased high test fuel and filled the tank. Water was added to the coolers. He checked the engine himself and found everything to be in good working order.

"Do you have any message for the governor of New York?" Fowler asked Governor Johnson. "Only yourself," Johnson replied, "You will be our best message from California." Without his mechanical crew on hand to clear space for take-off and spin the propellers, he relied upon those present for assistance. Governor Johnson himself spun a propeller and waved him off. Fowler took off at 5:50 p.m. from Sacramento, made a quick circle to wave at the crowd, and headed for the Sierra Nevada Mountains.

Fowler achieved his fastest airtimes of the day as he followed the railroad tracks into the foothills of the Sierras. The *Grass Valley Union* reported the following timetable: Between Sacramento and Roseville 18 miles in 19 minutes, between Sacramento and Loomis 25 miles in 25 minutes, an average of 54 miles per hour during the 35 minute flight. His total mileage for the first day of his transcontinental journey was 126 miles.

His first day's destination was the town of Colfax, where he planned to stay the night, but as he approached Newcastle, darkness began to fall. Unfamiliar with the terrain and not wishing to search for a landing site in the dark, he decided to land in Auburn. He circled the Placer County Courthouse to signal his unscheduled arrival.

Inside the cupola of the courthouse, three ladies were determined to get their first glimpse of the Cole Flyer and its handsome birdman. May Johnson, Mable Benhard and Cess Adams recorded the event in penciled graffito on the wall. It read " First airship through Auburn, Sept. 11, 1911."

After inscribing the courthouse wall, they rushed downstairs to announce that Fowler appeared to be making a landing on an open field at the old Collins ranch near the cemetery about a mile west of town.

Fowler was grateful when his biplane rolled to a stop. The time was 6:30 p.m. and it was nearly dark, but he could make out the shape of a man approaching on horseback. On the grassy hills near the town of Colfax, large crowds of people who had gathered to witness Fowler's historic arrival gloomily gathered their picnic baskets and began making their way back to town. Disappointed today, they would very soon have a chance to become part of history.

When word reached Fowler's hometown of Gilroy that he had safely reached Auburn, a cheer rose up from one end of town to the other. Thomas Fowler, still in San Jose, sighed with relief and climbed wearily into his car for the drive back to Gilroy. One day down, nineteen to go.

CHAPTER THREE

THE HIGH SIERRA

The San Francisco and Sacramento newspapers as well as the *New York Times* continued to follow his progress as the days wore on, but no coverage would be more complete than that of the *Grass Valley Union*, a foothill publication with a keen interest in aviation. Fowler was the man of the hour.

Local aviation enthusiast and inventor Lyman Gilmore had primed the presses for extensive coverage by staying in aviation news himself. His Gilmore Airship Company, complete with stockholders, was developing several designs and had constructed at least one monoplane. At the time of Fowler's arrival in the Sierra foothills, Gilmore was nearly ready to make a test flight with a new engine. Extremely private, yet openly eccentric, Gilmore often made news just by showing up somewhere.

Fowler's crew and mother aboard the train caught up to him in Auburn around 7:00 Monday evening. He announced from Auburn that he would depart at 8:00 the following morning and would make a run directly for the summit without stopping at Colfax.

C.F. Grundy, Fowler's manager felt they should continue on board the Southern Pacific train and wait for Fowler in Reno. He took a few members of the crew and did just that. Frank Murray, chief mechanician and a former autobile racer, stayed behind with Bob to prepare the Cole Flyer for the next day. A guard was posted and a small campfire was made to ward off the frost.

Percy Root, an old friend drove up in his touring car and the pair left for the Freeman Hotel in Auburn where Bob would stay for the night. By the time they reached the hotel, reporters and admirers were converging upon the scene.

They asked questions and marveled at the aviator's apparent lack of anxiety over the change in landing sites and the monumental task before him the following morning. But none, not even Fowler, could grasp the enormity of the challenge of vaulting the Sierras.

The morning of September 12 dawned clear and chilly. Bob rose early and ate a hearty breakfast at the hotel. When Percy Root arrived to pick up Fowler and Murray, Bob was anxious to get underway. "Got to wait for the weather report from the summit," Murray reminded him on the way to the Collins Ranch where the Cole Flyer sat ready for take off.

Anticipating cold temperatures at high elevations, Bob was warmly dressed. He wore moleskin riding trousers, with his legs "encased in black bandages" the *Grass Valley Union* reporter noted. Over a shirt he wore a heavy sweater coat, a light Norfolk coat and finally a heavy chauffeur's coat. A thermal bottle of "beef tea" and a canteen of water were strapped within reach for good measure.

Fowler prepares for take off in Auburn. Courtesy Searls Historical Library.

Crowds had been gathering since 6:00. With a good report from Frank Murray that the Wright was ready to fly, Bob was ready to leave. Murray reminded him again that the weather report had not been wired from the summit. Critical information regarding temperature, wind speed and direction would be helpful in planning his airtime and fuel consumption rates.

The 8:00 hour arrived with no report. Growing impatient, Bob sent a messenger back to town to find out what had happened. The messenger returned and informed Fowler and Murray that there was still no word.

They waited until 9:30 and Bob decided to take off, with or without the report. After handshakes from Murray and Root, he climbed into the seat and readied himself for take off. The crowd, whose anticipation had built to a frenzied level, could hardly be contained.

The Wright left the ground and was circling overhead to gain elevation when the much-awaited wire finally arrived in the hands of a breathless messenger. It read:

"FOR GOD'S SAKE TELL THAT FLYER
TO STAY WHERE HE IS ITS BLOWING
A GALE AT THE SUMMIT"

Murray and Root exchanged looks and raced for the car. There was, of course, no way to signal him, but they would be as close behind him as possible if they were needed. News reached the foothill towns eleven minutes later that he had flown over the village of Applegate, establishing a rate of one mile per minute.

He passed over Colfax at an elevation of between 600 and 1,000 feet and headed up Blue Canyon to the right of Cape Horn. The north fork of the American River glistened off to the right, and things were looking good for a run at the summit. As he climbed along the mounting Sierras the air currents became erratic, keeping the aviator busy just maintaining level flight on course, but it was nothing he couldn't handle. As he advanced up the increasingly steep grade he stayed above the tracks of the Southern Pacific Rail Road, his "iron compass."

B.F. Howe, a lookout for the forest service watched through field glasses as Fowler flew from Auburn toward the Sierras. He noted that Fowler's course was straight and true as he passed by at a fast rate of speed at an elevation of about 800 feet.

Bob directed the Wright over the mountain station at Alta with its small collection of houses and a general store. He noted that the ground was heavily shadowed by tall pines and other trees.

A sudden wind gust followed by a rapid down-draft tossed the light craft to and fro. Bob gripped the controls fiercely and worked furiously to maintain his course. But as the currents leveled off he discovered that something was wrong. The vertical rudder at the tail of the biplane was not responding to the stick. He could still warp the wings, but had no way to steer right or left. Further, a magneto wire had become disengaged which meant that he could not turn off the engine or even reduce his speed. With virtually no control over the aeroplane, he was simply a passenger.

He scanned the foothills for a place to land and located one meager opening in the pines where, with perfect control and some luck he might be able to set her down. Unfortunately he had neither.

He raced toward the clearing at more than sixty miles per hour. He had one chance to land but he'd have to pancake it. As the craft sank lower in its approach to the opening, two tall pines standing about forty feet apart loomed before him. With the Wright's wingspan at about thirty-nine feet, he'd need a miracle to thread that needle, especially with no rudder control. Bob braced himself and gripped the sticks.

He could feel the craft drifting right as man and machine hurled toward the patch of meadow grass. Would the Wright make it safely between the pines? He wouldn't wonder for long.

The right wings clipped the tree on the right with a splintering smash and the Wright was hurtled into the tree on the left with another violent impact. Still forty feet above the ground, the Wright flipped over and began to tumble downward, rear rudder first.

Still clinging to the sticks, Fowler fought to stay in his seat, the only thing between his body and the heavy engine. His view was of the sky, with the Wright at his back, careening toward the ground tail first. The rudder, tail section and

propellers splintered against the earth with a thundering crack. Bob was thrown from his seat directly against the engine, then out the back of the craft through the debris of the tail and rudder. He landed with a jarring thud on the pine needle-strewn ground of the clearing. The tranquility of the remote forest surrounded him as the enormity of what had just happened began to sink

Local resident George West snapped this photograph a few hours after the crash. Courtesy Ed and Charlene Fontana. Drawing previous page courtesy Sacramento Union.

in. The only sound was the intense ringing in his ears. He sat up, wincing at the jolt of pain in his back.

He looked toward the Cole Flyer--or what was left of it. Looking more like a gargantuan dead moth than an aeroplane, it lay belly up, wings crumpled and torn, landing gear pointing skyward, wheels still spinning. Fowler groaned as he struggled to his feet, then laughed aloud. The Cole Flyer was demolished, but somehow he had saved the landing gear.

The female station agent at Alta had seen the Wright hit the trees and disappear from sight. She rushed to the clearing and found Fowler with his goggles pushed up on his forehead, lifting a wing to look underneath.

"Is anyone hurt?" she shouted on the run.

"I don't think so." Fowler replied.

"We've got to get that airman out of there, where is he? she asked, arriving breathless at his side.

"You're looking at him, Ma'am."

The astonished woman offered to wire a message on Fowler's behalf, and within minutes the wires were buzzing from coast to coast with the following phrase:

BIPLANE WRECKED FOWLER SHAKEN BUT UNHURT

Fowler was met at the crash site by local resident Arthur Towle, who insisted that he take Fowler to the nearby Alta Sanatorium for a medical examination. Fowler's mother and crew had been notified, but it would be a few hours before they could make their way back down to the crash site to put together a

*Parts removed by a local resident while the Cole
Flyer was left unattended following the crash.*

plan of action. Fowler agreed to have a doctor check his back
and the painful bruises that were beginning to surface on his
body.

Mr. Towle returned to the biplane an hour later to discover
that local residents, turned souvenir hunters, had learned of
the Cole Flyer's location and were dismantling the aircraft piece
by piece. One young man was working on removing the propeller
and another a wheel from the landing gear assembly. Pieces of
cloth, wood, and the barometer had already been taken by others
when Towle arrived.

The *San Francisco Chronicle* declared: Towle "gave the
relic hunters some very plain talk about stealing, and it had the
effect of saving much that might otherwise have been carried
away." Arrangements were made for a guard, and Towle returned
to the sanatorium to check on the famous aviator. In his absence
Percy Root and Frank Murray arrived at the scene, learned of
Fowler's condition and whereabouts, then began to survey the
damage.

Murray concluded within the hour that although it looked
very bad, the Wright could indeed be rebuilt with spare parts on
the special train and a new rudder from the Wright factory in
Dayton. Fowler had, after all, managed to save the engine and
landing gear. Fowler would later say, of that attempted pancake
landing, that he "turned the pancake over."

Repairs got underway immediately and were the object of intense interest and scrutiny to the people of Colfax and surrounding communities.

CHAPTER FOUR

COLFAX COMES TO THE RESCUE

❧

With the exception of a wrenched back and deep bruises, Fowler's injuries were determined to be minor, and he convinced the physician at the Alta Sanatorium to release him the same day. He had to get back to his aeroplane. By mid-afternoon Faye Fowler and the mechanical crew, as well as manager C.F. Grundy had backtracked from Reno and met Fowler at the hospital. The crew was at the crash site and Faye and Grundy were trying to convince Fowler to stay the night at the hospital.

Fowler would accept nothing less than a ride back to the scene of the crash. The reporters, who were successfully kept away while the aviator was undergoing examination, mobbed him and his party as they left the hospital. Grundy watched Fowler, whom he still did not know well, and was awestruck at his reaction to the questions being fired at him.

Standing on the steps of the Sanatorium, Fowler smiled warmly and held up one hand for quiet. The statement that followed amazed everyone.

"I am sorry that the accident of this morning caused me to disappoint the people of Reno and towns en route who were depending upon my flying over the Sierra and across the state line today," he began. Going on to explain the technical aspects of the rudder failure and crash, he insisted that he would personally direct the rebuilding effort. "The accident to my machine has not stopped me. I'll fly to New York as soon as the damage has been repaired," he declared.

Fowler knew it was important to present a confident front and directly answer all questions if he hoped to keep the press

interested in the story. Foothill residents were overwhelmed by his humble statement. Fowler seemed more concerned about about their disappointment than his own monumental problems.

In New York, a 22 year-old aviator named Jimmy Ward had hastily prepared for a cross-continental journey of his own. With about one hundred supporters including his young wife to see him off, Ward departed from Governor's Island, New York at 9:08 a.m. on September 13, just two days after Fowler's start. Within a few hours he became hopelessly confused by the vast network of railroad tracks snaking out of Jersey City and followed the wrong one. He lost the better part of his first day trying to find the correct route.

The Colfax Rod and Gun Club, among its members prominent businessmen and other leaders of that nearby town, quickly met to discuss the aviator's predicament. James and William Keane, Dr. Dobbins, Carl Bell, Frank Durnin and John Butler decided that Fowler needed a place and money to repair his aircraft and that Colfax could use the publicity of having the celebrated coast-to-coast aviator in town for a few days. A preliminary show of hands confirmed that at least $250, maybe even more, could be raised from group members without a problem.

Durnin, Bell and William Keane drove to the crash site and met with Fowler. They would arrange for his lodging and meals, provide a place to rebuild the Wright and provide the cash in return for an exhibition flight prior to crossing the Sierras. Tickets sold for these test/exhibition flights would repay the funds, and both parties would benefit greatly.

Fowler accepted the committee's offer and arrangements were made to transport the aviator, his mother, crew and damaged aircraft into Colfax the afternoon of September 14 on Southern Pacific Railroad's Number 5 train. Fowler and his party were unprepared for the reception they received at the hands of the people of Colfax. The Colfax city band was playing a lively tune and the entire town turned out to greet them as they stepped off the train. Southern Pacific Railroad Superintendent Wood, also a member of the Gun Club, assisted in securing permission for Fowler and his crew to rebuild the Wright on a site in the center of town that had recently been cleared for a new roundhouse.

While Fowler supervised the unloading of his damaged aircraft, his mother was escorted to the Gillen Hotel, headquarters of the Gun Club. Some replacement parts which were on board the advance train waiting in Reno, Nevada, were immediately sent to Colfax and work got underway. The rebuilding effort became a source of fascination in downtown Colfax. Visitors came from surrounding communities for a look at the Wright biplane beginning to take shape in the dusty street. Fowler and his crew were hard at work during daylight hours

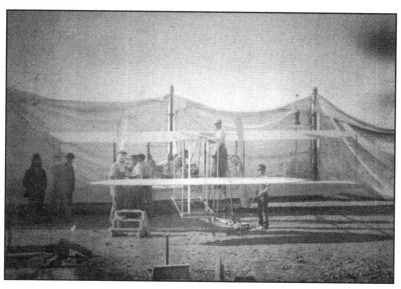

Lyman Gilmore at left. Fowler at center wearing white shirt and tie.

but always found time to shake hands with visitors and answer questions, many from children who were awestruck at the tall, handsome birdman and his remarkable airship. A canvas curtain at the rear of the site protected Fowler and his crew from dust and wind as they worked hurriedly to complete the repairs.

The *Oakland Tribune* reported on September 17 that the shattered biplane was already on its skids and wheels and that the wings, patches having been painstakingly sewn by Mrs. Fowler herself, looked nearly as good as new. The engine was already in place and the propellers were fitted into position that day. A completely new tail section, however, ordered from the Wright Aeroplane Company in Ohio on the day of the crash, still had not arrived. Fowler's hopes of taking off for the Sierras on Sunday, September 17 would have to be postponed a few days.

There was to be no shortage of excitement in the town of Colfax early that morning, however. At 3:00 a.m. Fowler was awakened by his mother pounding on the door of his room in the Gillen Hotel. A fire had broken out in the nearby Mountain View Hotel and all hands were needed. Fowler threw on pants and a shirt and rushed to the scene of the blaze. He worked with firefighters until a railroad tanker car arrived about thirty minutes later to put down the blaze.

John Wesley Dugger, a guest, died in his room in the hotel. Local resident Henry Hurst, who had run from door to door alerting sleeping guests, became trapped by flames and jumped from a second story window, breaking both legs and sustaining fatal internal injuries. "Fowler Fights Fatal Flames

at Colfax" the *San Francisco Chronicle* reported, praising him for his calm demeanor in the face of disaster, and cementing his role as a true friend of the people of Colfax.

On that same day in Sheepshead Bay, New York, a third contestant was just beginning his own cross-country odyssey. Calbraith Perry Rodgers, a Pittsburgh native whose family tree boasted such historical greats as Commodores Matthew Calbraith Perry and Oliver Hazard Perry, was seeking his own place in the history books. Backed financially by the giant Armour Meat Packing Company, Rodgers was completely outfitted for the journey with a newly-built Wright Model EX, a slightly smaller racing version of Fowler's Model B. Rodger's aeroplane, supplied by the company and christened *Vin Fiz*, was named for Armour's newest product, a carbonated grape drink.

Rodgers would receive five dollars per mile along the way, and his sponsors would pay for the special train (complete with Pullman car and hangar car) and its staff, up to a maximum of $40,000. Rodgers would pay for his own mechanical crew and any repairs and parts needed along the way. So, with his trademark cigar clamped in his teeth, Rodgers winged away to the west, headed for Los Angeles. His mother and wife were comfortably accommodated in the Pullman Car following the *Vin Fiz*.

Back in Colfax, Fowler used the extra time to study the weather conditions and patterns in the Sierras. Puzzling air currents and downdrafts were of particular concern and Fowler resolved to get as much information as possible before attempting

the difficult flight. He made several railroad journeys over the summit to locate prospective emergency landing sites, and measure temperatures.

The frustration and pressure must have been extreme forces during this time in Colfax, since he knew that Ward and Rodgers were now in the contest and already on their way. Every day that passed in Colfax meant one less day to make it across the continent within the allotted time. Fowler never showed a sign of irritation, but maintained an optimisic exterior. His mother and father, always supportive of their son, helped with arrangements and his mother Faye accompanied him to social events, chatting happily with the press whenever the opportunity arose.

Fowler was the man of the hour in Colfax with more invitations than he could accept. He worked daily with boxing trainer Tim McGrath, using a Corbett wrist exerciser to strengthen his wrists for the arduous flight over the Sierras. Wrist strength was essential to aviators. If muscle fatigue set in partway through the mountains, it could be disastrous since wing warping, steering and elevation were all controlled with hand-operated levers.

Grundy, his manager, had begun anew to apply pressure to move the starting point to Los Angeles and bypass the Sierras completely. As the days in Colfax passed, Bob grew firmer in his conviction that he owed it to his supporters, the people of the foothill communities, to continue his course from there and, in his words "vault the Sierras."

During his time in Colfax, local amateur aviator Lyman Gilmore visited the reconstruction site at least once. Nervous stockholders of the Gilmore Airship Company offered Fowler, a far more experxienced aviator than Gilmore himself, a chance

Lyman Gilmore, standing at left next to unknown boy. Fowler is at center. Note that Fowler has fitted the Cole Flyer with a "cocoon" (directly in front of Fowler) to protect his legs and midsection from wind and cold at high elevations. Courtesy Nevada County Historical Society Newsletter.

As final preparations are made for the first flight, Fowler and mother Faye are seen standing at left center looking toward the men crouched in the foreground.

Faye Fowler stood by her son throughout the difficult days in Colfax.

to test Gilmore's experimental aircraft. Fowler politely declined, citing his own full agenda. A few days later, while Gilmore was revving up the new 35 horsepower engine for the test flight, the crankshaft snapped in two, shattering the engine. Surprisingly no one was injured by the shards of flying metal, but local headlines proclaimed "GILMORE'S ENGINE REDUCED TO ATOMS."

On Thursday, September 21, the long-awaited tail section and rudder had finally arrived on the afternoon train. Fowler and his crew had everything else ready, and once the new parts arrived, they had the aircraft completely reassembled in a few hours. A trial flight was scheduled for 9:00 a.m. on Friday, September 22. The Narrow Gauge Company rearranged its train schedule to run special excursions so that residents of the foothill communities could attend the trial flights.

Everything was prepared that morning as Fowler and crew arrived at the makeshift hangar in the center of town. Clear skies and only a slight breeze gave promise of great things to come. New equipment was counted among the additions to Fowler's rebuilt Cole Flyer including a new aneroid barometer for measuring altitude, a compass, an automobile watch affixed to one of the uprights and Fowler's newest innovation, a cocoon of canvas to protect his legs and lower torso from cold and wind. Among his new supplies were spare tires, a tire pump strapped to an upright and a 125-foot length of rope. Experience thus far had shown him the damage spectators could inflict on his delicate machine. He figured he'd hand the rope to spectators who would form a circle, maintaining a safe perimeter around the aircraft. He would find this to be among his most useful articles as time went on.

More than 300 spectators arrived on the narrow gauge railroad to witness the much-anticipated test flights from Colfax. Many more arrived by automobile, wagon and on horseback, with picnic lunches and field glasses to make the most of the day. Local schools called an official holiday so that students could attend the festivities.

Fowler started the Wright's engine and found it to be running well. It was then turned off so a few minor adjustments could be made. Fowler gave instructions to the event staff charged with clearing his take off path. Exchanging a nod with mechanician Ralph Newcomb, Bob shook hands with each member of his crew and kissed his mother. He climbed into the seat and positioned his legs inside the cocoon. A quick check of

Test flights on September 22, 1911 proved to be thrilling for the loyal residents of Colfax, who had supported Fowler and his party for ten days.

Hundreds of excursionists from neighboring towns joined residents of Colfax to witness Fowler's test flights and wish him well.

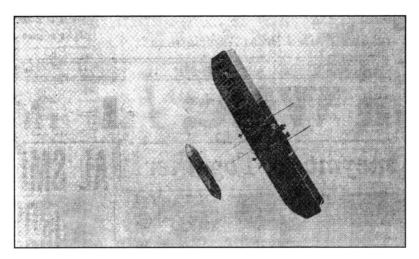

A newspaper photographer snapped this photo as Fowler circled over Colfax during his test flight/exhibition. "R.G. Fowler/Cole Flyer" is painted on the underside of the lower wings.

his instruments confirmed that all was ready. Everyone but the crew stepped away. He signaled them to spin the propellers, listened to the stacatto clack of the chains through the guides, then nodded for the men at the tire blocks to pull them out. Last, he signaled for the holders to let go. The Wright surged forward and raced down the field, lifted off smoothly and soared upward. The crowd began to cheer as the wheels left the ground. After being grounded for ten days, Fowler and his Cole Flyer were finally airborne.

He circled several times over the town, then flew her a distance away to see what she could do. Upon returning to Colfax, he remained cautious, and performed no daring maneuvers, but thrilled the crowd nonetheless. His complete control of the aircraft and graceful turns mesmerized the onlookers, whose eyes never left the biplane until Fowler brought her in for a smooth landing in almost exactly the same spot from which he had taken off. As the wheels touched the grass, the crowd again went wild, cheering and slapping backs. As Fowler stepped from the machine, his mother rushed forward to kiss him. "She's running splendid," he told his crew, grinning, "and we'll soon top those almost insurmountable Sierras all right."

Fowler had agreed to make an additional exhibition flight late in the afternoon. It too went off without incident, and Fowler declared himself and his plane ready to take on the mountains

A landing at Carpenter's Meadow

the following day. A reporter for *The Day in Grass Valley*, marveling at Bob Fowler's level-headedness and bravery, wrote "..Fowler will continue his journey over the Sierras, pawning his life in the game of progress..."

While Friday, September 22 was a great day for Fowler, aviator James Ward was not so lucky. Plagued by engine problems in each of his five days competing for the Hearst prize, Ward crashed again. At his wife's insistence, he withdrew from race for good, his expenditures for repairs having exceeded $22,000. Competitor Cal Rodgers was faring no better in his cross-continental bid. Like Fowler, he crashed on his second day out, the "Vin Fiz" sustaining heavy damage. Rodgers escaped serious injury, and was extracted from the wreckage still puffing on his lighted cigar.

Fowler and his crew made arrangements for an early morning take off the next day, hoping he could get over the Sierras before the perplexing midday air currents could take hold. Large crowds were on hand, and at 6:43 the Cole Flyer took off with a heavily dressed Fowler at the controls. Faye Fowler had traveled ahead by train with manager C.F. Grundy to meet her son in Reno, his first scheduled stop.

Fowler circled a few times to gain altitude and headed over Cape Horn, Gold Run, Dutch Flat, Towle and Midas to Blue Canyon. He reached an altitude of 6,000 feet above sea level, but could not make any headway against the winds and downdrafts. With a groundspeed of only 8 miles per hour, he was nearly flying in place. Fowler decided to return to Colfax and replace the motor with a more powerful one. He landed at 8:55 a.m. A pioneer who had crossed the Sierras in the Gold Rush days was among the first to greet him as he stepped from the Cole Flyer and pushed his goggles up on his forehead.

"Young man," he declared, "I had to fight for my life to get over those mountains on foot, and I don't think you're going to ride over on a rod of sidewalk with a laundry wagon for a tail."

After a quick assessment, Fowler and his mechanical crew discovered that the original motor from the Wright factory had two extra teeth on the drive sprocket which would save motor revolutions, causing the motor and the propellers to turn more slowly than necessary. They checked the spare motor they had rented from the Wrights and discovered that it did not contain the two extra sprockets. The extra RPMs in the spare motor might be just what the Cole Flyer needed to make it over the hump. The motor was exchanged, and plans were made for a 5:30 start on the morning of September 24.

Weather reports supplied by various members of the Colfax Rod and Gun Club stationed near the summit (elevation 7,088 feet) said skies would be clear and winds would be from the southwest at 15 miles per hour. Fowler's observations the past ten days had taught him that the wind did not become a major force until after 8:00 a.m.

"Might as well shoot her," he was heard to say. The Wright took to the air at daybreak, complete with the rental motor.

Fowler followed the previous day's route, achieving an altitude of 8,200 feet above sea level-plenty of altitude to fly over the summit. It was slow going, requiring full throttle just to maintain his altitude and a little forward momentum. It took one hour and 42 minutes to reach the town of Cisco, 18 miles from his goal. Here he experienced his first trouble. Intense wind gusts and unstable air created a hole or funnel, and Fowler found himself falling 300 feet within seconds. He recovered his altitude, but the replacement motor was laboring under the extreme conditions. A combination of problems contributed to what happened next. The cooling system in the Wright engine was inadequate given the strain it was under. The fuel mixture had been leaned out to allow the maximum performance to reach the required altitude. At full throttle, this caused the engine to overheat.

The motor quit abruptly at about 8,000 feet, and Fowler with his hands full in gale force winds trying to keep the Wright from being thrown against the nearby peaks, was too busy to attempt to restart the engine. Remembering a clearing he had seen, he circled back about 5 miles to Carpenter's Meadow, a small field just outside Emigrant Gap at an elevation of about 5,200 feet above sea level. He volplaned into the small field for an emergency landing in unstable winds, snagged a landing gear wire and damaged one skid while making an abrupt stop.

19th century meets 20th century in Carpenter's Meadows as the Cole Flyer awaits repair of a damaged landing gear wire.

Fowler (right) and new friends try to keep things light as tension builds and time runs out in the Sierras.

He was fortunate to find himself right beside the railroad tracks with a "helper" engine headed back to Colfax nearby. The crew saw him land and asked permission to stop the engine and assist the celebrity aviator. He rode back down to Colfax where his crew and repair materials were still waiting with the special car to be hitched to the next northbound train. The special car with parts was taken up to Carpenter's Meadow a short time later and side-tracked. Fowler and crew secured rooms at a small hotel near Carpenter's Meadow and began to make the repairs.

"The water in my radiator was simply boiling," Fowler said later to reporters, "I had no choice but to descend." Besides the landing gear wire and broken skid, the motor would require some adjustments based upon its performance that morning. His mechanics were also debating whether to replace the radiator as an additional precaution.

A make-shift repair camp was assembled, but weather reports predicted rain the following day that would continue for about 18 hours. True to the forecast, light rain mixed with occasional snow flakes fell during most of Monday, September 25th, and the crew worked busily in dropping temperatures. Good weather was predicted for the morning of the 26th, but repairs and adjustments would not be complete until too late that day to attempt the crossing. Fowler had learned a lesson about late starts and the accompanying dangerous winds.

The Wright was sharing the field with three horses, three cows and "a rapidly changing throng of the curious," said the *Sacramento Union* on Tuesday, September 26, which also reported clear skies and perfect flying weather. The mechanics remained hard at work on the machine and Fowler remained resolved to get the aircraft over the mountains. A test flight late in the afternoon confirmed to Fowler that the Wright was responding to his every command. He told reporters that he was tempted to make a run for the summit right then, but with dusk approaching, he decided to take no chances.

More disappointment came at dawn the next morning. High winds were reported at the summit and heavy frost had formed on the machine overnight. The crew had to use hot water to melt the ice which had formed on the radiator. Arrangements were made for canvas to cover the aircraft that evening, and bonfires were lit in a circle to elevate the temperature near the biplane. Fowler hoped anxiously for calm, clear weather for Thursday, September 28.

The 75 mile per hour winds of the day before had calmed and weather conditions were perfect the next morning as Fowler and his biplane bounded down the field in a fresh start. He circled several times and reached 1,500 feet when the magneto began to cause trouble. He brought the craft down for an uneventful landing, giving reporters nothing more to write about but exceptionally good weather and Cal Rodger's progress in the midwest.

After solving the magneto problems, Fowler took off for a short test flight in preparation for a new start on Friday morning. Weather conditions were again perfect the following day. On take off into a mild breeze, the engine audibly misfired, and after only a brief low flight, Fowler brought the plane down, narrowly missing a wire fence. The landing gear wheel struck a mound of earth, buckling the wheel under the skid. The shattered wheel would have to be replaced. Other problems, which had necessitated the early landing included a leaking cylinder water jacket, a broken manifold belt and worn inlet valve springs. As repairs were getting underway, news came that a severe weather front was expected the following day which would bring low temperatures and snow to the Sierras.

Fowler and crew retired early that evening with a sense of dread and awoke to find a blanket of snow on Carpenter's Meadow and its uninvited guest. Even the optimistic Fowler had to concede that it would be impossible to continue the flight from there with winter weather upon them. The high altitude in the Sierras and the inadequate cooling system in the Wright motor combined to spell "impossible."

Fowler had a conference with his mechanics, all of whom expressed their desire to see the task through to the end. To a man they would stick with him. Having already used 19 of the 30 days allotted for the transcontinental journey, there were not enough days left to make it across the rest of the continent even if no problems were encountered. Fowler spent the day sending telegrams and making arrangements for a new start from Los Angeles.

"Better head south, boys." Fowler told his crew. Snow and ice in the Sierras made continuing the flight from there impossible. Mountain residents confirmed that conditions would only worsen as days sped by.

Above, Fowler readies himself for take off from the aviation field at Fremont Place and Wilshire Boulevard near the Los Angeles Country Club. Below, the Wright rises above the heads of spectators who watch with wonder as Fowler wings away to the east. Courtesy San Jose Mercury News.

CHAPTER FIVE

LOS ANGELES AND AWAY

❦

A refreshed and ready Bob Fowler took off from Los Angeles heading east on October 19, 1911 from the aviation grounds at Fremont Place and Wilshire Boulevard near the Los Angeles Country Club. The October 10 deadline for the Hearst aviation prize had passed, but Fowler was determined to achieve his goal. In a new start he aimed for Pasadena in the late afternoon, where a reception was sheduled in his honor. Cal Rodgers was still making his way west in fits and starts. A series of crashes had delayed him, but he too was determined to reach his goal, prize or no prize. Both aviators were optimistic that Hearst would award the prize anyway to the first man to fly from coast to coast, time limit notwithstanding.

Flying over Los Angeles a fog bank moved in and Fowler lost his way. He found himself above Whittier when the first clearing came, and had to circle back to the northwest to find Pasadena.

Word of his departure reached Pasadena's Hotel Maryland where Mrs. Fowler and friends were waiting. They rushed to Tournament Park, his designated landing site. As darkness approached, Faye Fowler listened anxiously for the sound of her son's engine. The fog had lifted, but the increasing darkness would be just as perilous.

In the seat of the Wright, Fowler gripped the controls, scanning the ground for a familiar landmark. He knew he must be over Pasadena and was circling in the darkness. A white square caught his eye. He steered closer and dropped lower. A white bed sheet spread on the ground with a lantern placed at it's center was his runway marker on the dark polo field.

Faye Fowler, in one of her finest moments, had heard the Wright's engine long before any of her companions. Insisting to her doubtful friends that she could hear it, she gave orders to clear the field. Soon the engine could be heard clearly as the aircraft began to circle. She realized that Bob could not make out the polo field in the darkness. On her orders the bedsheet and lantern were located and set at the center of the field. He made a perfect landing in complete darkness.

"There's class to that sheet," he grinned as he hugged his mother close after stepping from the aeroplane. Later at the reception, he announced "I will take off my hat to my mother. Her action was unexpected and certainly was a clever thought. When I saw that white spot the effect was thrilling, for I had just been wondering how I would determine where to alight. The oiled surface of the polo field made all the surroundings look dark and the sight of that sheet was like an oasis in a desert." If the press had wondered about the origins of Fowler's resourcefulness and nerve, their wondering was over.

The next day was wasted in Pasadena while manager Grundy tried to bully Fowler into restarting at Venice Beach where an incentive purse had been raised. Fowler refused to concede to the ultimatum, stating that he would either "continue from Pasadena or quit." He argued that restarting for financial or any other reasons would make a sideshow of his effort, and with a successful start under his wings, he would continue.

Yuma, Arizona

At that, Grundy threatened to sieze the plane-technically still the property of the Cole Motor Company-if Fowler took off for the east. Fowler returned to the Hotel Maryland and waited while Grundy and his associates conferred. They finally agreed that the flight would continue on from Pasadena as originally planned. Evidently the agreement contained the provision that Grundy be replaced as manager. Norwood R. Cooper was hired as the "front man," his only purpose being to manage public relations. Fowler would be in complete control of his transcontinental flight from that time forward.

It had been widely reported that Fowler's journey had come to an end, and most people were surprised to hear that he took off for the east on the morning of October 21. By October 26th he had reached Yuma, Arizona and was enthusiastically greeted by residents of that town who had never seen an aeroplane or an aviator before. Fowler was the first to bring an airplane under its own power into the state of Arizona (one had previously entered the state loaded on a boxcar). A bronze plaque bearing Fowler's image was later dedicated in Yuma to commemorate this historic event. After leaving Yuma, he set an American aviation endurance record, four hours and twenty-six minutes of sustained flight (167 miles) between Yuma and Maricopa, Arizona.

Coast-to-coast rival Cal Rodgers was making steady progress in his east to west flight, and was scheduled to reach Tucson, Arizona shortly after Fowler on the first day of November. It was too momentous an opportunity to miss, and although it would mean a short delay, Fowler decided to wait for Rodgers. He landed the Cole Flyer on the campus of the University of Arizona and damaged his skids and one upright after a wind gust threw the machine into a fence. Fowler waited for Rodgers, who landed off campus a short time later.

The competitors shook hands and Fowler wished Rodgers well. Rodgers congratulated Fowler on his record-breaking flight a few days earlier. Rodgers, his ever-present cigar still clenched in his teeth, was impatient to get back into the air. He ate lunch and promptly flew off for Maricopa. Bob now understood why the nation had not "warmed up" to Calbraith Perry Rodgers. Any joy (and Fowler doubted even this) Rodgers had taken in his protracted flight at the beginning was obviously gone. Visibly exhausted, Rodgers wanted only to finish it. Without allowing his mechanics time to make substantive repairs, Rodgers took off from Tucson at 2:51 p.m. He was forced down a short time later at Maricopa, his engine leaking copious amounts of oil.

Fowler stayed overnight in Tucson for minor repairs and scheduled a take off for 8:30 the following morning. He arrived without incident at Benson, Arizona, and by the fifth of November was winging his way through New Mexico toward El Paso, Texas. It was evident that Rodgers, barring disaster, would be the first aviator to complete a coast-to-coast flight, being only a few days away from Los Angeles. Fowler's flight was personal now. Completing it would be his minimum measure of success.

CHAPTER SIX

MAROONED IN NEW MEXICO

❧

With the wind at his back this day, he had flown a respectable 114 miles in just 82 minutes. The steady roar of the 32 horse power motor assured him that the unpredictable contraption was at least firing on all four cylinders. His only link to civilization was the thread of railroad tracks below, his "iron compass." The tracks had guided him thus far, and should see him the rest of the way to the east coast. "I'm still in the middle of nowhere," thought Fowler, but at least trains passed by a few times each day. Far ahead, he glimpsed the Rio Grande River, marking the border between New Mexico Territory, the U.S. state of Texas and the nation of Mexico. He was nearing El Paso, Texas, where he would stay for the night and fly an exhibition the following morning.

It had been a difficult take off from Hachita that morning. Starting the motor was a substantial challenge at an elevation of 4,514 feet. Twice his mechanicians had to alight from the waiting railroad car and assist with start-ups. The train's crew waited patiently as Bob's crew adjusted the motor. When at last he and the Wright were in the air, Fowler steered in a wide circle over the locomotive to signal that all was well. He headed toward the east and was on his way. The Wright's engine had run smoothly, as it was known to do on rare occasions, and a 30 mile per hour wind was at his back. This was a welcome break after the two previous days of battling in-your-face wind gusts throughout the state of Arizona. His wrists were still sore from the day before.

The sight of the Rio Grande fueled his confidence, and it occurred to him that November 5, 1911 would be a fine day to break another record. He spotted a mass of rocky hills in the distance; the railroad tracks snaked their way through. By increasing his altitude and flying in a straight line, Fowler could shave additional minutes off his flight time. It would mean leaving the tracks for a bit, but he would rejoin them just beyond the hills.

He steered a few miles to the south, just across the Mexican border. Surveying the landscape he observed a profusion of towering cathedral cactus, mesquite and Spanish bayonet plants scattered amongst golden sand dunes and an occasional jagged hill. Not an airplane-friendly environment, but on this, the 18th day of his second attempt at the transcontinental prize, he'd seen worse.

Suddenly, POP! A valve blew in the engine and Bob Fowler's heart sank. His flying was over for the day. A few sputters later the motor cut off completely. With a firm grip on the sticks, the aviator changed direction and brought the plane under control. Wrists aching, he fought to land the plane with little propeller speed.

The Wright's 39-foot wing span was again a liability as he searched the desert for a suitable landing site. He knew that the wings would be shredded by the giant cactus if he passed too close, and the desert's other plantlife would be none too helpful either. At last he spotted a small patch that was relatively clear, but it would take some finesse to fit the Wright into it. Fowler worked hard on the levers, and steered directly into the 30 mile per hour gusts to cut his forward speed. Courtesy of the wind, he lowered the aircraft to earth almost like an elevator. The Wright touched down on the desert floor, and rolled twenty feet to an abrupt stop with one landing gear wire snagged on a hearty Spanish Bayonet plant.

"The Lord gives us our relatives, 'tis said.
Then it must be the devil gives us our forced landings."
-Robert G. Fowler

Fowler climbed from the rigid seat and surveyed the landscape, surprised at the remoteness of his location. He covered the motor with a spare piece of canvas and muttered an oath for having strayed from the railroad tracks. His rapid flight eastward had put him two hours ahead of the special train carrying his crew. The tracks were about a mile and a half to the north of his "landing site." If he hurried, he could meet the train and still get to El Paso by dinnertime.

The terrain immediately surrounding his plane was sandy, but quite firm. He began to hike northward through sagebrush, cactus and rocks, and was already working out the details of the next day's take off when his boots began to sink ankle-deep into soft sand. Fowler had brought the Wright down, it seemed, on the only solid ground for miles. This put a new twist on the problem.

Dripping with perspiration, Bob Fowler reached the tracks, and was just collecting his thoughts and his breath when the eastbound train came chugging down the tracks toward him. He stood, cap in hand, and waved his arms madly to signal the engineer to stop. The engineer smiled broadly, waved back, tooted the whistle and roared past.

Bob sat down in the sand, put on his cap and laughed incredulously as the train disappeared around a curve. His mother, he knew, would send out the alarm soon enough. She was already waiting in El Paso, and when he didn't arrive on schedule there, she would arrange a search. Since Bob and his entourage had left Pasadena, Mrs. Fowler had filled various roles as provisions manager, promoter, and provider of moral support. He didn't relish the thought of waiting in the desert until someone found him, but there was no other choice.

Luck once again was on Fowler's side as he rested near the tracks of the El Paso and Southwestern Railroad that afternoon. A few moments after passing him, the train's engineer remembered seeing Bob on the platform that morning in Hachita. Realizing that the man beside the tracks at Mastodon was the famous aviator, the engineer stopped the train and backed up to let Fowler board. He'd been picked up by the train before anyone was aware of the forced landing. Bob joined his surprised crew on board and explained the job before them. The fourteen miles to El Paso passed quickly as Fowler and his group made plans for a repair and take off the next day.

Everyone was full of optimism as they hopped off the westbound train the next morning and trekked out to the marooned biplane. As he surveyed the terrain with a critical eye, it was obvious to Fowler that some clearing and grading would be needed to permit a clean take off. Fixing the motor was simple enough. The damaged cylinder was removed, the valve replaced. Newcomb and Sutro fine-tuned the engine and replaced the landing gear wire. Meanwhile, twenty volunteers from El Paso and a railroad crew on their day off set to work with shovels, picks and gloved hands clearing a crude runway. A steady wind lashed the canvas-covered planes, and airborne sand pelted the faces of the men charged with getting the Wright off the ground. At last the largest growth was removed, and the ground leveled a bit. Pointing at some soft spots, Fowler directed the volunteers to trample down the earth as best they could. Otherwise the wheels and skids would sink and he'd never get the aeroplane up.

"It don't pack down, Mr. Fowler," a local worker informed him after several minutes of work on one powdery spot. Bob conferred with crewmen Ralph Newcomb and Adolf Sutro, who were becoming accustomed to Bob's "creative" ideas. After some quick calculations, an order was hastily sent to El Paso for giant bolts of heavy duty canvas. The day was already spent, and everyone boarded the eastbound train to town.

Another restless night was spent in El Paso as Bob contemplated the the newest take off plan. When they hopped off the train on the morning of November 7th, they brought the makings of a new runway. Facing directly into the savage wind, bolt after bolt of the fabric was carefully arranged and staked to the ground to form a runway twenty feet wide and one hundred twenty feet long. The tedious operation took all day, and it was late afternoon before the runway was in place. With darkness falling, take off would have to wait for morning. Another valuable day had come and gone. Bob and his entourage wearily gathered up their tools and boarded the eastbound evening train at the spot they'd dubbed "Fowler's Landing."

The morning sun was just easing over the horizon on Wednesday, November 8th as Fowler, Newcomb and Sutro pulled the aeroplane into place at the end of the canvas runway. The wind, however, had shifted overnight. Situated in its current direction, the runway was useless since the wind was gusting at a right angle to the sprawling bipane. So they waited, and at last nature chose to cooperate with their take off plan. Around noon, the wind shifted back to the previous day's course. Without delay, Bob climbed into the seat of the aeroplane and readied himself.

With its engine roaring, the Wright seemed as anxious to begin as its pilot. All fingers were crossed except Fowler's, who gripped the controls with white-knuckled intensity. Bob gave the signal and Sutro and Newcomb let go. The wheels dug in, the machine sank a few inches, and at first it appeared that the Wright was moored to its spot. Fowler increased power and the craft lurched forward in a clumsy roll. The aeroplane's weight and the instability of the underlying sand made it impossible to get up to take off speed. Each time Fowler pushed for more speed, the wheels dug in deeper and forced the canvas down into the sand, slowing him down. It was no use.

Exhausted more from frustration than exertion this day, Bob organized a makeshift camp in the desert for himself and crew. Sleeping under the stars would certainly beat "commuting" back and forth to El Paso. Bob pledged that the next time he arrived in El Paso, it would be by air, not by rail. The group built a bonfire to ward off the chill of the November night, and basked in the camaraderie of men allied in a venture to achieve a common goal. A night of rest brought to Bob Fowler a new idea for getting the Wright off the ground.

Local workers had passed word from Bob to his mother Faye, who was staying in El Paso. Included was an order for lumber to be dropped at Fowler's Landing the following morning. Faye Fowler managed the duties of arranging food and supply deliveries to the camp and visited frequently to check on the progress of the laborious operations. By the end of the fourth day in the New Mexico desert, the Wright had been not-so-fondly-dubbed "GROUNDHOG."

Along with breakfast on the morning of Thursday, November 9, came delivery of an order of lumber. The young aviator was amazed to observe yet another group of volunteers jumping off the train and unloading boards. Some members of the El Paso crew were repeats at the camp, but there were many new faces as well. At least twenty workers had reported each day since his forced landing. The volunteers set to work arranging boards end-to-end, in line with each wheel of the biplane. They had just enough for a 100-foot stretch of plank runway—not much, but long enough if conditions were favorable. Yesterday's canvas was laid out at the end of the wooden track for good measure. Everything seemed ready.

Hopeful eyes turned toward Bob and his reluctant aircraft on the morning of Friday, November 10. The aviator took his place at the controls and steeled himself for take off. The engine roared as he bumped along the runway. He coaxed as much engine speed as possible in the short distance available, but was still shy of take off velocity as he reached the end of the last plank. But there was still the canvas. The wheels rolled onto the cloth, and the Wright immediately began to slow down. There just wasn't enough traction on that canvas. Disgusted, Bob cut the motor and rolled to a mushy stop.

By the time his group met him at the far end of the runway, numerous ideas were circulating about what to do with the biplane. Bob didn't feel like hearing any of them. The endless delays were costing not only precious time, but resources that would be needed to complete the cross-country race. Fowler feared that his crew might lose faith in the project. Then where would he be? He tried to push aside in his mind the reality of "an unbeatable combination" of a weak 30 horsepower engine trying to lift a 800 pound aeroplane off the ground with no runway traction at an elevation of 4,200 feet above sea level.

Finally Adolf Sutro approached him with a suggestion. Why not dismantle the machine and transport it by rail into El Paso where Fowler could take off from solid ground? He could then backtrack by air to meet the race requirements, fly over Fowler's Landing then continue on his way across the continent without further delay. Bob considered this, but did not relish the idea of arriving in El Paso with his unassembled aircraft on a railroad flat car. The townspeople had already waited five days since his promised arrival on November 5th for their first sight of an aeroplane. That first glimpse should be up in the sky, he asserted, not on the platform of a railroad station. Discouraged, Fowler retired early to his tent, opting for the oblivion of sleep over a fireside evening with his crew. For the first time since the start of their journey, Fowler's troupe had no game plan for the following day.

After a fretful night, the aviator awoke before dawn on November 11 with an unbelievable idea. He rushed to the tent of Sutro and Newcomb and shook them awake. They listened with bleary-eyed incredulity as their young employer outlined his plan. The two mechanics exchanged looks, tried to maintain their composure, then burst out laughing. This was certainly the most incredible scheme to date. For more than hour both men attempted to persuade Fowler not to try it.

By mid-morning, Fowler had convinced Newcomb and Sutro that the idea was just crazy enough that it might work. Bob believed in it, and that was enough for them. The mechanics knew that if they didn't demonstrate unswerving support for the plan, then nobody else would.

The plan went something like this: the Wright would be disassembled into three sections and hand-carried to the tracks, reassembled, then lifted onto a railroad pushcar, which was simply a small platform on four wheels which ran along the tracks. The engine would provide power to the propellers, which would in turn move the pushcar down the tracks, hopefully achieving the 40 miles per hour needed for take off. He could then pull down on the elevator lever, lift off and be on his way.

Arrangements were made for a push car and some extra wooden ties. The crew began dismantling the Wright. Fowler directed the operation as the planes were partially dismantled for transport to the tracks. The center section of the aeroplane with its landing gear was alternately rolled and shoved clumsily across the dunes—a very slow process. Adding to the exhaustion of the work was the misery of a sudden wind storm which, on several occasions, threatened to tear up or blow away the lightweight planes. Airborne grains of sand bombarded their eyes, making the task even more difficult.

By the end of the day, the camp was relocated track side. Weary crew members secured the Wright with rocks and tools as the wind whipped fiercely. During the long night, Fowler and his crew took turns on watch as the fragile aeroplane was buffeted about in the sand.

Thinly-veiled skepticism was the prevailing mindset of the crew. During two days of moving operations, many of the El Paso volunteers sought private moments with Fowler to dissuade their new friend from attempting his ambitious plan.

Fowler (left), his crew and helpers take a break from pushing the Wright through the desert sand. Bottled "Poland" drinking water was a necessity in the New Mexico desert. Courtesy San Jose Mercury News.

Bob, however, was very pleased with his idea and believed he could bring it to fruition. When repeatedly warned that it would not work, he smiled, shook hands, slapped backs good naturedly and returned to his work. He knew better than anyone that this plan *had* to work. It was surely his last option if he hoped to bring the Wright to El Paso by air.

Morning dawned calm and bright, but the pushcar did not arrive from El Paso. There was a mixup, and by the time it reached Fowler's Landing, it was too late in the day to attempt take off. The 7th day in the desert ended in frustration, and without progress. Another windy night passed and at sunup everyone awoke to a calm breeze from the southwest. Word had spread throughout the region of Fowler's plan to launch his aeroplane from the El Paso & Southwestern railroad tracks, and unusually large groups of helpers began arriving on the scene. Local and national newspapers reported the details of Fowler's take off plan with mixed predictions.

That evening came word that Cal Rodgers had suffered serious injuries in a crash at Compton, California, just a few miles short of his goal—the Pacific Ocean. His Wright model EX was completely destroyed in the crack-up. Although he was expected to survive, Rodgers remained unconscious with injuries including a broken ankle, concussion and massive bruises. It was unknown whether he would ever fly again. Rodger's crash meant that although the Hearst prize time limit had passed, Fowler was still in the race.

Lifting the Wright onto the pushcar proved difficult. The span of the aircraft's landing gear skids was substantially wider than the pushcar platform. Two railroad ties were placed fore and aft atop the platform, providing the width needed to support the aeroplane. The craft was situated to keep the Wright from sliding off, yet allow it to ascend when sufficient ground speed was reached. When the unwieldy contraption was at last balanced upon the ties, everyone stood back to look it over.

Most doubted that this top-heavy "flap jack stack" could make it even twenty yards down the rails without tipping over. Certainly secret bets were riding on the predicted outcome of Fowler's experiment. Bob supervised and continued making plans for the take off. If he was nervous, he wasn't showing it.

At last planted in the seat with hands gripping the controls, and goggles in place, Fowler called for Newcomb and Sutro to start the motor. The engine sputtered, caught, then rumbled to life. But it was limping badly—not the sort of performance that would bring the 800 pound aircraft off the push car at high altitude. Fowler cut the motor and climbed from the seat as his assistants steadied the Wright on its perch. Newcomb and Sutro were already studying the motor. In moments, Ralph had located the trouble. "Magneto's full of sand," he called to Bob.

A short time later, the engine was declared sound, and Bob once again took his place at the controls. This time, the engine ran smoothly, even at full throttle. This was it. A wave of excitement coursed through the assemblage as everyone took their assigned places. Two railroad section hands stationed some distance down the tracks were charged with derailing the pushcar after takeoff.

Above the thundering of the engine, Bob shouted last minute instructions and reminders to his crew, then muttered to himself, "Better hurry up, Fowler, someone else might want to use these tracks."

He coaxed the four cylinder motor to full throttle, let it roar for a few moments, then signaled the ground crew to begin a running push. The outfit lurched forward as the propellers moved the craft forward. The pushcar wheels slowly began to turn on the rails. Fowler felt the aeroplane and pushcar buck against one another as each fought for equal momentum. At last the outfit stabilized as real forward motion was achieved.

Bob drew in a deep breath and grinned. The motor was running fine and the dual-action contraption was actually beginning to pick up speed on its approach to a gentle curve. As planned, a slight incline in the tracks helped him gain speed more rapidly. It was working. But when he reached 30 miles per hour, the pushcar began to shimmy and vibrate. With its short wheel base, the pushcar was neither designed nor proportioned

Preparing for take off, the Wright, with Fowler at the controls, is perched atop the push car.

to travel at high rates of speed with a top-heavy load. For take off, Bob would have to coax it to at least 40 miles per hour. The aviator looked down to study the stability problem. So far the pushcar was holding to the rails as it came around the curve.

He brought his head up, took a look down the tracks, and what he saw made his heart stand still. Headed directly toward him about a half mile distant and closing quickly, was a freight train chugging down the same track he was on! It was the biggest locomotive he'd ever seen, its shining headlamp staring him in the eye.

The instinct of the seasoned race car driver took hold, and Bob went for the brakes. But of course there were none, and no way to stop the contraption now speeding down the tracks. He glanced at the section hands standing at the ready to derail the pushcar. He was now traveling at about 35 miles per hour. He hoped that the section hands wouldn't panic and derail

To an observer from another era, this incident would have looked like a "Coyote and Roadrunner" cartoon. Pen and ink drawing by Marci Bishop.

the pushcar before he and the Wright could take to the air. To derail the pushcar and plane at that speed would be disastrous to both aircraft and pilot.

At that moment, the engineer at the controls of the freight train saw the plane racing toward him. He blew the whistle one long blast followed by several shrill short ones, and shut down the throttle. It would be quite some distance, however, before the train could make a complete stop. For good measure, the engineer leaned his head out the window and waved his arm wildly, adding yet more emotion to the chaotic scene. Fowler made a split-second decision. He'd have to try for a Hail Mary take off, and bail out at the last minute if it failed. He worked at the controls and tried to lift off, but found that he still needed more ground speed. The locomotive was getting larger and larger. Fighting the instinct to bail out of his seemingly doomed aircraft, Fowler waited a few more critical seconds, then jerked hard on the elevator lever and felt the wings gulp the air.

The plane was flying! Flying forward, yes this was good. But flying just a few feet above the pushcar, without climbing! This was not good. He was still on a collision course with the locomotive nearly upon him now. In order to climb up and out of the way, he needed air speed. Bob leveled the wings again and aimed directly at the headlamp of the locomotive.

At last the aircraft surged forward with a burst of speed, and again Bob jerked forcefully on the elevator lever. The stubborn aeroplane rose up, clearing the smokestack of the massive locomotive by just a few feet.

Bob Fowler looked down the throats of the train's hollering engineer and fireman. Just ten feet above the train now, he was close enough to see that the engineer's tonsils had been removed!

A glance over his shoulder revealed that the section hands had successfully derailed the pushcar, and were jumping up and down slapping backs. The train had almost completely stopped on the tracks. Bob took a deep breath, gripped the controls and made a wide circle overhead to signal his thanks. To an observer from a later era, this take off would surely have looked like a "Coyote and Roadrunner" cartoon.

Fowler finally flew over El Paso, Texas at 11:40 a.m. Monday, November 13, 1911, and was greeted by a large crowd as he landed on the infield of Washington Park. It had taken eight days to achieve the infamous take off. Deluged with requests for interviews, the aviator observed that if the take off had to cost eight miserable days, then at least it had earned him some publicity and the nickname "Handcar Bob."

Courtesy San Jose Mercury News.

"Little drops of water,
Little grains of sand,
Make gasoline poor fuel
And send me down to land."
-Fumings of Fowler, 1911
The Daily Picayune
New Orleans, Louisiana

CHAPTER SEVEN

THE SOUTHERN ROUTE IN WINTER

❦

Lying ahead of Robert Fowler was a journey through the center of the giant state of Texas, the approximate mid-point of his transcontinental flight. Following the lengthy delay in New Mexico, Fowler's flight took on a new direction. Largely cut off by the Cole Motor Company after the dismissal of Grundy as manager, financial obligations became a factor. The cost of supporting a mechanical crew full time and providing fuel and parts for the Wright had to be given a number one priority. Exhibitions were the most lucrative way to finance the completion of the journey, and Fowler siezed the opportunity.

Further, it had become apparent that the northern route, with an ending in New York was impractical because real winter weather had set in in the northeast. Fowler had had enough snow on his wings while held up in the Sierra Nevada Mountains. It was decided that after steering north to Fort Worth, "Fowler's Flying Circus" as it had become known, would head south and proceed to the Atlantic through Louisiana, Mississippi, Alabama, Georgia and Florida. It was a time of many changes for Fowler and his crew.

Manager Norwood R. Cooper left the group during their journey through Texas, and Charles L. Young came aboard as the new manager and "front man." Young was a friend from Gilroy, California who was completing his recuperation from an illness at the Houston Hot Springs. He had been following Fowler's progress across the continent, and sent his wife and a driver to meet the aviator at his landing site near the town of Cypress, Texas. Young was immediately signed as Fowler's new manager. Young, not affiliated with the Cole Motor Company or any of its agents, was enthusiastic and full of new ideas. He brought with him a head for business and fearless ideas for promotion and publicity that immediately breathed new life into the Fowler group. The original crew had stood by him in even the most difficult times, and vowed to continue with him all the way to the Atlantic. Faye Fowler, too remained by her son's side and traveled with the special car as it zigzagged through the south.

Stops in Texas included Sierra Blanca, Van Horn, Pyote, Sweetwater, Abilene, Fort Worth, Corsicana, Cypress, Houston, and Beaumont. At Iona, just outside Fort Worth a blown spark plug forced Bob down in high winds in the midst of a herd of steers. The stampeding cattle came very close to the fragile aircraft, but disaster was avoided.

During much of Fowler's travels through Texas Cal Rodgers was recuperating from his injuries at the Hotel Maryland in Pasadena. The *Vin Fiz* was completely demolished, and a new aircraft was being assembled; the only original parts resurrected were the tail elevator, the vertical rudder and the two propellers. Fowler remained hopeful that he himself would be the first aviator to fly from coast to coast, but Rodgers was determined to finish first. Although his ankle would still be in a cast, Rodgers scheduled the final segment of his flight for December 10, 1911.

Taking off from Van Horn, Texas on November 19, 1911. Courtesy San Jose Mercury News.

Fowler at the controls in Beaumont, Texas with E.R. Shaw, aerial photographer in the spare seat. Courtesy San Jose Mercury News.

Fowler arrived in Fort Worth on November 29, where 50,000 tickets had been sold for an exhibition at a baseball park. High winds delayed him several times along the way, but he reached Houston on December 3.

Heading east, he reached the city of Beaumont, Texas where Fowler created another aviation first. Taking motion picture photographer E.R. Shaw with his camera aloft in the spare seat, Fowler facilitated the first-ever aerial motion pictures. Wet conditions on the ground and the added weight of a passenger and camera made it difficult to rise into the air, but after making several adjustments, they got off the ground. He was under contract with the Champion Film Company of New York and the Beaumont Chamber of Commerce, and pulled off the work without major incident. Headlines blazed from New York to Pasadena with news of the aerial motion pictures as well as Fowler's prediction that in a short time aerial photography would be a substantive aid in surveillance of enemy military positions.

While Bob was filming and waiting for clear weather in Beaumont, Cal Rodgers became the first aviator to fly from coast to coast. He landed his newly rebuilt EX on the sand at Long Beach, California on the tenth of December after an uneventful fourteen minute flight. More than 50,000 spectators witnessed the end of Rodger's historic journey.

Bad weather, unlike any the region had experienced in the previous ten years retarded Fowler's progress from Beaumont. It was eight days before he was finally able to attempt a flight to Lake Charles, Louisiana. On December 21 he made his way to Jennings, Louisiana in time to record another aviation first.

"I made the first medical delivery by air
of Typhoid serum
from the little town of Jennings,
Louisiana to Evangeline."
-Robert G. Fowler

Bob spent Christmas Eve, 1911 with a family of strangers, Mr. and Mrs. Funk of Paradis, Louisiana, when a spark plug failure forced yet another unscheduled landing in a rice field covered with 18 inches of water. Telephone communications in the small community were cut off each evening at 6:00 p.m. and there was no way to get word to his group as to his whereabouts. A tense Christmas Eve passed for his mother and crew who had traveled ahead by train and were waiting at New Orleans.

Bob chats with cowgirl Alberta Claire, known as "The Girl from Wyoming" who with her dog by her side had ridden from coast to coast on horseback. San Jose Mercury News.

Foul weather during the rest of December made it impossible for Bob to reach New Orleans until the afternoon of New Year's Eve. Using a railroad pushcar to take off for the second time, he narrowly missed telegraph wires along the tracks. The aviator arrived in New Orleans on the first anniversary of the death of aviator John B. Moisant and flew over the crash site and Moisant's burial place in Metairie Cemetery. Local reporters marveled at Fowler's courage in flying over such an infamous spot on such an anniversary in the face of a forty mile per hour gale. He brought the Wright in for a smooth landing at the City Park Race Track and stepped from the seat grinning as usual.

Fowler and his party passed three days in New Orleans while rain pelted the Gulf Coast. Observers in New Orleans noted that the Wright clearly showed signs of the punishment inflicted during the flight up to that point, most notably the wings, where added metal strips reinforced wooden ribs and thousands of autographs darkened the fabric. The group planned a quick flight through Mississippi as landing sites in the southern part of the state were few. The city of Biloxi raised a small purse and arranged a landing site to induce Fowler to make a stop on his way to Mobile, Alabama. Arriving in Biloxi in the afternoon of the fifth of January, Fowler's mood seemed to match the weather he had been battling for the past month. "Owing to the recent rains the country is practically all swamp" he reported, "The weather is very cold to fly now and my fingers are frost bitten from yesterday's flight."

Five foggy, rainy days were passed in Biloxi and Fowler finally left the city on January 10 at 11:00 a.m. heading for Pascagoula and Mobile. He circled Pascagoula at a height of 300 feet and aimed northeast toward Mobile bucking a strong head wind. He landed in Mobile, Alabama around 1:00 p.m. and left the Gulf Coast a few hours later for Flomaton, a small town near the border of Alabama and Florida. The first day of good weather in more than a week boosted spirits, and Fowler and manager Young arranged a race between the train and the biplane. Fowler would give Young aboard the train a one hour head start, and Fowler would try to overtake him on the way to Flomaton. Fowler and the Wright arrived ten minutes before Young and the train.

Except for a minor propeller repair in Georgiana, things went along fine until Fowler reached Brantley, Alabama on the 20th of January. A brief landing and visit was uneventful, but

Flomaton, Alabama

The crash at Brantley, Alabama which caused a 15 day delay and $1,000 in damages. Courtesy San Jose Mercury News.

on take off, a wind gust threw Fowler off his path and his landing gear collided with a series of tree stumps, causing $1,000 damage and a delay of two weeks. Residents of Dothan, 60 miles distant, who had collected a purse for an exhibition stayed in communication with the Fowler camp. They were anxious to know the progress of the complicated repairs, and on which day Fowler would arrive in their city. But Bob was a veteran of numerous forced landings and delays, and did not want to disappoint Dothan residents by setting a time and being unable to live up to it. On January 23, 1912 a frustrated Bob Fowler issued the following statement to *The Dothan Eagle*:

"Look for me when you see me coming"
-Fowler

He finally left Brantley, Alabama on the 5th of February, made a visit to Troy, where he donated a broken propeller to S.H. Blan, editor of the *Troy Messenger* who had extensively covered Fowler's journey to that point. The propeller was placed among other relics in the office of the *Messenger* so visitors could look at it. Fowler crossed the border of Georgia on February 6th and visited the towns of Donaldsonville and Bainbridge where he spent the night. During nearly every flight Fowler contended with spark plug problems. He took off for Thomasville, Georgia the next morning and made it to Quitman before calling it a day.

February 8th, 1912 would be a day that Fowler would never forget. He left Quitman, Georgia and gave an aerial exhibition over the town of Greenville, Florida. He landed at Live Oak to refuel and perform one more brief exhibition. His goal in sight, Fowler took off as soon as the Wright had been thoroughly checked. An 82 mile flight across the southern tip of the Okefenokee Swamp lay ahead of the exhausted aviator and his worn out biplane. It was late afternoon when the citizens of Jacksonville were alerted that Fowler would be arriving that day by air to cap off his transcontinental journey.

Manager Charles L. Young had arranged Fowler's arrival to coincide with a two-plane air meet taking place at the Moncrief Park Race Track in Jacksonville. Aviators Max Lillie and Harold Kantner were sent out by Young to meet Fowler in the air and escort him to the park. The crowd went insane with excitement when at 4:30 p.m. the drone of the two engines became audible. Fowler circled the field three times, executed sev-

An exhausted Robert Fowler guided the Wright to a graceful landing on the infield of the Moncrief Park Race Track in Jacksonville, Florida on February 8, 1912. Courtesy John P. Ingle Jr.

Left to right: World champion wrestler Frank Gotch, Max Lillie and Robert Fowler. Courtesy John P. Ingle Jr.

eral dips and spiral dives over the crowd, and brought his battered biplane down for a textbook landing. Lillie and Kantner alighted nearby and rushed to introduce themselves to their brother aviator who had just completed such a monumental task. City officials handed Fowler the key to the city and told him:"go as far as you like." World champion wrestler Frank Gotch was also on hand to greet Fowler and offer his congratulations.

Manager Charles L. Young and Robert G. Fowler shaking hands at center. Courtesy San Jose Mercury News.

Fowler was nearly frozen, completly exhausted and infinitely grateful to be relieved of the pressure of the transcontinental journey. He was soon whisked away by automobile to Jacksonville's Seminole Hotel where he enjoyed the excitement of the moment and waited for his mother and crew to join him for a much-deserved celebration. Although he had landed in an Atlantic coast city, he still wanted to roll the wheels of the Wright in the surf to complete his mission.

For the next few days, while Bob and his party were basking in the completion of their Herculean task, manager Charles L. Young was attempting without success to line up sponsors for the final few miles of the journey. Fowler made the decision that with or without sponsorship, he would fly the last hop as soon as the Wright was overhauled. On February 17, 1912 he and the Wright took off from Jacksonville, flew 15 miles and landed on the sand of Pablo Beach, Florida. The waters of the Atlantic lapped at the tires and skids as Fowler, stiff with cold, climbed from the seat and embraced his mother. "I knew you would make it, Bobby," she exclaimed tearfully. "I knew you would."

Bob would later describe the personal qualities that saw him through the arduous transcontinental flight as "ignorance, courage, humor and a complete lack of fear."

"I knew you would make it, Bobby," exclaimed Faye Fowler as she embraced her son at the Atlantic shore on February 17, 1912. Courtesy San Jose Mercury News.

The four cylinder motor that powered the Wright Model B during Fowler's transcontinental flight. The motor is now on display at the Hiller Aviation Museum in San Carlos, California.

Robert G. Fowler's 1911-1912 transcontinental flight facts:

-45 actual days of flying
-121 calendar days from start to finish
-96 spark plug changes
-65 forced landings (an average of one for every three flights)

PRICE 10 CENTS : : : PAY NO MORE
OFFICIAL PROGRAM
SAN FRANCISCO'S
International
Aviation Meet
TANFORAN AVIATION FIELD
DEC. 25 to 29---1912
TOM GUNN
BEACHEY

CHAPTER EIGHT

PANAMA

❦

The excitement of the end of his journey began to wear off and Fowler, still frustrated that Rodgers had been the first aviator to fly from coast to coast, began looking for his next challenge. He spent some time in Florida and Georgia working the exhibition circuit, but began to feel homesick for his native state of California.

On April 3, 1912 Cal Rodgers was killed instantly when he crashed a Wright Model B into shallow surf at Long Beach, California. He died a few feet from the spot where he had completed his transcontinental flight nearly four months earlier. Witnesses stated that a flock of seagulls flew into the path of the biplane, and Rodgers was forced to dive at a steep angle to avoid them. Working hard at the controls, he tried to pull up, but was too close to the water. A strong tail wind contributed to an already rapid dive, and the biplane smashed violently into three feet of water. The engine broke free and crashed into the aviator's back, breaking his neck.

Financial concerns prompted Robert Fowler to fly exhibitions and fairs during most of 1912. The overhauled Wright Model B lost its "Cole Flyer" nickname and again read simply "Robert G. Fowler" on its underwings. He spent much of July in Overland Park and Kansas City, Kansas flying exhibitions. He met and began a friendship with a young woman named Josephine Conway of Kansas City. Josephine was either widowed or divorced, and had two daughers from the previous marriage. Fowler spent as much time as possible with her be-

Fowler (at right in balloon gondola) at the Mars-Fowler Aviation Exhibition in Overland Park, Kansas July, 1912.

fore leaving Kansas to fulfill obligations in other places. Aviation was his passion, and everything else would take a back seat to that pursuit.

During August he was the main attraction at Iowa's Jefferson County Fair. Officials thanked him for his contribution to the financial success of the fair, and extended wishes that Fowler's "careful manly work may help to bring about a practical use of the air for practical aviation." His role as "the careful aviator" had clearly been cemented. More exhibitions at the Old Settlers Picnic at Orleans, Nebraska kept him busy through the end of August.

Fowler competed in the San Francisco International Aviation Meet at Tanforan Aviation Field in December of 1912. He broke the altitude record for northern California with a flight of 9,100 feet. But daredevil pilot Lincoln Beachey was the thriller

Above: Josephine Conway captioned this photo of herself on the wing of the Wright "Going up for altitude." Bob took it with him when he returned to California that fall.

Lincoln Beachey and his Aeroplane in which he looped the loop ©

Daredevils like Lincoln Beachey were grabbing headlines with death-defying stunts. Beachey's skill made them look easy, and many exhibition pilots died trying to imitate his famous maneuvers.

of the show, performing his repertoire of aerial stunts such as the Dutch Roll, Loop the Loop, spiral dives, upside-down flying and more. Beachey's fearless antics were crowd-pleasers, but Fowler was the solid, dependable contender who had proven his tenaciousness in completing the coast to coast flight earlier that year.

The intense competition of the exhibition circuit was not Bob's favorite environment, and he seemed to consider participation in such events as a necessary evil. He was amazed at the mindset of the spectators, who seemed hungry for a disaster at every meet. Swept up in the thrill of danger, they cheered wildly when the most dangerous maneuvers were attempted. When a pilot crashed, (not an uncommon occurrence) spectators had been known to rush to the scene and sieze souvenirs from the mangled wreckage or articles of the aviator's bloody clothing even before offering assistance. In discussing this "lust for souvenirs," reporters could not resist making the comparison between such spectators and vultures siezing upon a carcass.

Six months of exhibition work convinced Bob that it was time to seek a greater goal. He found it in a non-stop coast to coast crossing of the Isthmus of Panama. By September of 1912 Bob was yearning to get back to California and get started. While completing exhibition commitments in Kansas City, he began working on plans for a new, more powerful aeroplane with Jay Gage, a Los Angeles aeronautical engineer and aviator whose aircraft designs were getting a lot of attention. Bob placed an order for a single propeller tractor biplane with an enclosed fuselage, which would make flying in adverse conditions more comfortable. The propeller, located at the front of the aircraft "pulled" the plane, as opposed to "pushing" the plane as the twin rear props had done in the Wright's design. A V-8 A-3 Hall-Scott 80 horsepower marine engine insured the needed power to achieve Fowler's newest goal. The engine had been heavily tested and promised to make frequent spark plug failures and overheating a problem of the past.

Jay Gage had set up a factory and flying school at Los Angeles' Griffith Park aviaton field just as Fowler was completing his cross-country tour early in 1912. By September he had produced his fourth airplane. Fowler's would be his fifth. Gage and Fowler collaborated on its design, taking care to manufacture it in sections which, when dismantled, could be easily crated to fit into the hold of an ocean freighter. The design of the new aircraft included a passenger seat situated in front of the pilot's seat. This extra seat would be essential as Fowler planned to

Left, a handbill from a hometown aviation event. Right, Bob prepares for an aerial inspection of power lines for the Western Power Company in December, 1913.

JAY GAGE
AVIATOR AND AERONAUTICAL ENGINEER
FLYING TAUGHT. BUILDER OF THE GAGE BIPLANE
320 EAST 5TH STREET

LOS ANGELES, CAL. _Sept 3 1912_

150 S west 5 st Glendale

Mr R. G. Fowler
Kansas City

Dear Friend I received your letter today but I didn't get your telegram. Will start immediately on your plane and am sure I can have it done for you by Oct. 1st and would like to have the motor radiator. and truck by the 21 or 22. I can space the planes 4' 6" just as well as 4' and it will make just as neat and good a job. so I will space them 4' 6". I make a regular passenger seat which can be put on or left off. I place passenger seat in front of operator directly over center of pressure so it makes no difference in the balance of the plane with either one or two. a twenty five galon gas tank would be all right but it would make a much neater looking plane with about a 10 gol. tank for exhibition work and then have a larger one for your cross country work I am glad you sent me your weight. I will sure see that the plane

Letter from Jay Gage to Robert G. Fowler outlining details of the construction of Fowler's new airplane. Fowler, whose varied flying experiences during the previous year had taught him a great deal, specified numerous changes to Gage's design. The result was a fast, flexible aircraft adaptable to nearly any environmental condition.

JAY GAGE
AVIATOR AND AERONAUTICAL ENGINEER
FLYING TAUGHT. BUILDER OF THE GAGE BIPLANE
820 EAST 24TH STREET

LOS ANGELES, CAL.

flies O.K. before sending it to you. I forgot to
mention I received your check of $400.00 as
deposit on plane. thanks. the way I have
been making my wings is as per sketch.

(could be cut here) lower wing   (could be cut here)   upper wings

now they could be cut at dotted lines and they would
crate 5 ft. 3 in. by 6 ft. 3 in. and if you wish me to do so
I will cut them, the way they crate now is 5 ft. 3 in. by
12 ft. 3 in. over all. I rather like the idea of having the
wings in as few parts as possible. the only draw back is
convenience in shipping. Francis is making good
and I understand he has had no trouble with his
chains. did your chains ever give you much trouble
I have a double tractor that I have been using for
about 7 months in the school and we have had very
little trouble so far with our chains. hoping to hear
from you again soon and thanking you for
your order. I am very truly yours
Jay Gage

Fowler's plan to ship his new airplane to Central America for a
non-stop crossing of the Isthmus of Panama created special challenges in the construction of the craft. Dotted lines indicate where
the planes could be cut for crating. Note the design of this craft
incorporates upper planes with a greater span than the lower
planes. Fowler's Wright Model B had upper and lower planes of
equal span.

reprise his role carrying a motion picture operator. This time they would capture aerial views of the magnificent Panama Canal under construction.

Bob had heard of pilots who planned to fly over the canal but, stymied by wind and weather conditions, never attempted the flight. The April 1912 edition of the *Aero Club of America Bulletin* included an article titled "Why We Did Not Fly Across The Panama Isthmus" by *Collier's Weekly* photographer James H. Hare. This article must have been of particular interest to Fowler, who was considering making his own flight across the isthmus at the time of the article's publication.

Hare, who was accompanied by a pilot and Al Welsh of the Wright Aviation School, outlined the financial aspects of the trip to the canal zone, and noted the perils of the severe crosswinds. Additional risks of a trans-isthmian flight included a complete lack of landing sites along the route. The floor of the canal, still not filled with water, was too rough to land upon without wrecking an airplane, and was bordered on each side with dense jungle. Further, workers (about 42,000) were swarming everywhere setting off charges of dynamite, which would make a forced landing additionally hazardous. The Wright machine brought by Hare and his team to the canal zone in 1912 must have been similar to Fowler's Model B. Welsh felt strongly that the unreliable motor was another cause for concern. Fowler, citing his own engine experiences during the transcontinental flight could hardly disagree. The editor of the *Aero Club of America Bulletin* concluded that once the canal was filled with water, the crossing would be far less dangerous to pilot and machine as pontoons could be installed on the airplane and a landing could be made on the water of the canal if necessary.

Fowler was aware of the obstacles, but by December of 1912, he was ready to try it even though conditions in the canal zone had not changed measurably since Hare's report the previous spring. Fowler had great confidence in his new aeroplane with its powerful state-of-the-art motor. He began in earnest preparing for his flight across the Isthmus of Panama during winter and spring of 1913.

A commercial partnership was formed between Fowler and the Gaumont Moving Picture Company of Paris for motion pictures of the Canal zone to be taken by cameraman Ray Duhem while riding in the passenger seat of the biplane.

Studying everything from weather patterns to canal construction updates, Fowler primed himself on conditions, routes

*Fowler tests his new "Fowler-Gage" airplane at Los Angeles'
Griffith Field in the fall of 1912.*

Fowler and Duhem testing the Fowler-Gage in San Francisco before affixing the pontoons for the Panama flight.

and possible hazards. He arranged for wooden pontoons to be affixed to the Fowler-Gage, converting it into a hydroaeroplane. No one knew better than Fowler himself what he faced. Having flown nearly three thousand miles during his transcontinental flight, he knew that it would be easy to underestimate the dangers of what seemed like a simple task--a 52-mile flight.

Fowler contacted the War Department in Washington and secured permission to fly over the canal zone. Since previous attempts at the flight had failed, it must have seemed unlikely to War Department officials that Fowler would succeed either. Bob also contacted Colonel George C. Goethals, U.S. military commander in the canal zone, and discussed his plans for the flight. A year later, in a court of law, Fowler would quote Colonel Goethals as stating "I have never placed any obstacles in the way of any of the other fliers who tried it, so would hardly do so in your case, besides there is nothing here we don't want you to see."

The difficulties of transporting the new airplane via ocean into a foreign port were substantial. As weeks advanced, Fowler checked off solutions to each problem presented, and quickly added a new one to take its place. Just a few days before the planned departure in April he learned that the high-test fuel his plane required was not available in Panama. He hastily made arrangements with the Union Oil Company for 50 gallons to be shipped on one of their tankers. The Union Oil tanker was scheduled to leave San Francisco for Panama just hours ahead of the steamer *Pennsylvania* carrying Fowler, the plane, his crew and cameraman Ray Duhem. The 3,000-mile trip from San Francisco to Panama aboard the aging *Pennsylvania* took more than two weeks. A severe wind storm off the coast of Nicaragua created very rough seas, making the trip even more uncomfortable. By the time the ship docked in Panama, Fowler and his party were weary of sea travel.

As sections of the plane were removed with care from the hold of the *Pennsylvania*, Bob discovered that his fuel, transported in tin cans aboard the Union Oil tanker, had evaporated when heat in the cargo hold caused the seams of the cans to rupture. Fowler put his head to the task of securing fuel and his crew made arrangements to transport the plane to the nearby beach that would be the base of operations. The Fowler-Gage was carefully inspected and found to be no worse for wear from the rough sea voyage. The aircraft was reassembled and fine-tuned. The Panama Fire Department generously donated 50 gallons of their high test fuel-imported from New York regularly-and it began to look at last like the flight might be possible. The base of operations on the beach presented its own set of challenges for the crew.

"One big trouble on the beach I had set up
as base was the large tide movement. At this point
there was a 30 foot tide change-when the tide was out my
plane was a quarter of a mile from the water."
-Robert G. Fowler

Preparing for the trans-isthmian flight on the Panama side.

Fowler in white slacks working on the Fowler-Gage while Duhem (in passenger seat) prepares his motion picture camera for the flight.

They quickly learned that flights would have to correspond to tide movements or the plane (on pontoons, not wheels) would have to be pushed and shoved a quarter mile through the sand to reach the ocean for take off. Test flights, essential to ensure that all parts of the plane were functioning at 100 percent, began a few days after arrival. The first was a short hop over the Bay of Panama. A short section of motion picture footage was taken so that Duhem could adjust his camera to local conditions in preparation for the crossing a few days later. The first test flight was uneventful, and after landing the motor was adjusted according to Fowler's instructions. Duhem reported that he had encountered no problems with his camera or film and that he would be ready when Fowler was.

The second test flight a few days later began at high tide with a 20 mile per hour wind kicking up 3 foot waves on the bay. Bob got the plane off the water without trouble, but in his first turn into the wind about 150 feet off the ground, the motor sputtered. He leveled the plane to pick up speed and coax the engine. The wind promptly died and the plane made a sudden drop toward the ocean. He needed air speed to keep the nose of the plane up for the unscheduled landing or the pontoons would dig into the waves instead of skimming along the top and the plane would do a somersault. As they dove rapidly toward the waves, Bob urged the motor into one more little burst of speed that brought the tail down slightly. The pontoons hit the water and knifed through the waves. Bob managed to keep the aircraft from somersaulting forward, but the propeller hit hard dislodging a piece of copper sheathing and scooping water up and onto the motor, dousing the carburetor. The motor stalled. Ray stopped his camera and turned to look at Bob.

"This left us stopped in the water in a bad spot.
Ahead of us was Chirique Point, a rocky head-land
lined with rough coral reefs just below the water's surface
--all the while the wind at our backs was carrying us
nearer disaster. So I had to hurry to try and
restart the motor to make a getaway from
our hazardous position."
-Robert G. Fowler

Time was not on their side with a strong wind carrying the plane and its two occupants toward Chirique Point. Duhem, who was a cameraman, not a crewman, had no experience starting airplanes, but was quickly indoctrinated. With the damaged propeller Bob knew he could never get enough speed for take off, but they could taxi the plane the half mile along the surface of the water to shore. Bob removed as much water as possible from the carburetor and gave hasty instructions to Ray who would have to spin the propeller to start the motor. The cameraman safely stowed his precious equipment and ventured out onto the two-foot wide pontoon. With only three feet of space in front of the propeller, he had little room to leverage himself and spin the blade.

The plan went something like this: Bob, who understood the engine would manipulate it while Ray spun the propeller. If the motor started, the plane would surge forward and Bob would scramble back to the controls. Duhem would dive sideways into the water to avoid being struck by the dangerous propeller. If he wanted a ride to shore he would have to grab a strut above the pontoon as the plane taxied by and haul himself into the passenger seat as there was no way for Bob to stop the plane short of stopping the engine again.

Incredibly, the startup attempt worked after five minutes. Duhem, his clothing soaked, heaved himself up and into the spare seat. Muttering an oath for not thinking of it before starting the plane, Duhem removed his restrictive wet clothing and sat back for the ride to shore. Two minutes later the engine sputtered and died again. Still too far from shore to signal for help, Duhem, now naked, stepped carefully onto the pontoon for a repeat performance. Three more times the pilot and cameraman restarted the engine. At last the plane taxied into shallow water and Fowler waded to shore. He gathered dry clothes for Duhem and sent them out to the plane via rowboat so the cameraman could make a decent appearance on shore. Duhem had certainly demonstrated to Fowler that he was a team player.

While making repairs to the propeller, it was discovered that an adjusting screw on the carburetor had jarred loose before take off that day, causing the plane to lose power. It was often the simplest mechanical problems that created the most difficult situations.

"As the rainy season was fast approaching
it was imperative that I get into the air
as soon as safety would permit."
-Robert G. Fowler

Bob and his party were anxious to get a look at the canal and the work underway, and even more anxious to break a record. Bob's preliminary research could not possibly have prepared him for the remarkable feat of engineering that he and Ray Duhem would witness during their flight. On the morning of Sunday, April 27, 1913 Robert Fowler and crew checked and rechecked all parts of the biplane looking for anything that might cause a disastrous forced landing on the still-unfilled canal bed. Ray Duhem had discovered while viewing the film exposed during the test flight that the vibration of the airplane was affecting the camera. He soldered some metal strips into place to close off part of the lens, allowing him to speed up the film by fifty percent. He was confident that it would solve the problem.

High tide had arrived, and when aviator and cameraman were ready, the Fowler-Gage was pushed into the surf and prepared for takeoff. Fair skies held the promise of perfect flying weather, but Fowler was aware of the capriciousness of nature in the tropics. They took to the air without incident, and headed immediately eastward over the Miraflores Locks. Heavy winds began to push the plane around, and Duhem found that he could not keep the camera trained on the ground or on any object and hope to get a clear picture. Fowler cut the engine speed so the partners could talk it over. Duhem agreed with Fowler that if they could increase altitude they might get clear of the heavy wind gusts. Fowler circled back toward the western coast and rose two thousand feet. The air seemed calmer and as they again headed east toward their destination of Colon on the Atlantic side and Duhem signaled that the camera was working fine. They made good time and soon reached the Culebra Cut, about one quarter of the total distance to Colon. Duhem kept

Workers pose for a photo near Gatun Lake as Fowler and Duhem fly overhead.

the camera rolling while Fowler observed with wonder the monumental task being carried out 4,000 feet below.

> *"The Culebra Cut [was] a scene of great activity-*
> *at least ninety steam drills were busy drilling holes*
> *in the mountainous rock--dynamite blasts popping off*
> *it seemed every few minutes. It was necessary to load*
> *the broken rock onto long trains which hauled it the ten*
> *miles to the Bay of Panama where it was being*
> *used to build a huge jetty connecting the*
> *Naos Islands with the mainland and making a useful*
> *breakwater protecting the Pacific entrance of*
> *the canal from any storm waters."*
> -Robert G. Fowler

Flying along over Culebra at about seventy miles per hour, the plane was suddenly jolted by a severe wind gust and completely reversed direction. Fowler and Duhem found themselves flying west again without so much as a twitch of the contols! At the same time, an air hole opened below them and they dropped a stomach-turning 300 feet straight down. "I had gotten onto a giant merry-go-round it seemed," Fowler explained later, "with no effort on my part." Turning back toward the east, Bob found himself wondering just who was at the controls of his plane.

Above Gatun Lake, a rain storm materialized and caught up with them. Duhem turned the camera around and trained it on Fowler to keep the huge rain drops which were pelting them in the face from damaging the camera. With his goggles wet and fogging up, Bob rested the control stick on his shoulder and carefully pulled out a handkerchief to wipe the lenses. Duhem kept the camera rolling. As the rain cleared they spotted the Gatun Dam and Spillway and the mile-long length of the gargantuan locks and approaches. Nearly at the end of their journey now, Fowler and Duhem flew over the town of Cristobal, the official port of entry to the Canal. Just beyond Cristobal was the city of Colon and the end of their flight.

Just as they were over the center of town the gas ran out. Limon Bay on the Atlantic side was within sight on the horizon, but Bob had become so preoccupied with the empty gas tank that he was focused on finding a suitable landing site. He lost 2,000 feet of altitude before remembering that his landing gear had pontoons, not wheels. Shooting for Limon Bay,

Success! An empty gasoline tank caused a forced landing in Limon Bay on the Atlantic Ocean at Cristobal. Landing amid coral reefs, one pontoon sustained minor damage. Ray Duhem is in the foreground with his motion picture camera on his shoulder.

bay would be the ideal spot for a landing but he would have to settle for something closer. Nearing the docks, he saw a dredged channel that would have to do. Just below the surface of the calm water he could make out coral, a real hazard, but his options were exhausted. He shouted for Duhem to brace himself and leveled the plane as best he could. At first contact the wooden pontoons glided smoothly, but then as the weight of the plane caused it to settle, a terrible bang followed by a scraping sound rose up. A huge gash had opened up in one pontoon, but at least they were down safely.

Duhem and Fowler looked at one another and grinned. In shallow water near a major city they were safe, and the Fowler-Gage was basically intact. Each had acheived his goal. Robert Fowler had made the first non-stop coast-to-coast airplane flight and Ray Duhem had made the first aerial motion pictures of the Panama Canal. They climbed from the plane and waded to shore.

Colon was quiet that Sunday afternoon in April, and little attention was given to Fowler's historic flight. But personal victory was enough for Bob Fowler. He and his group spent several days preparing the plane for shipment back to San Francisco, and answering congratulatory telegrams from friends and family. Colonel George Goethals was stunned to learn of Fowler's and Duhem's successful flight and contacted them immediately after they arrived back in Panama City. His tone more chagrined than congratulatory, he inquired as to what footage had been obtained and how they planned to use it. Goethals told Duhem that any films of the fortifications on Negos Island near Balboa on the Pacific side would have to be cut out. Duhem responded that until the film could be taken back to New York for development, he would not know what they had to work with.

"I suppose he (Goethals) thought we would never do it. I think his request is reasonable and I will submit the films to him at Washington later, so that he can see what the result will be. Of course I can see the justice of his position, and I don't want to be a party to giving away the government's secrets." Fowler told reporters on May 9. The successful flight stirred a flurry of activity in Washington D.C. in the weeks that followed. If an airplane could fly over the Canal and shoot motion pictures, then the zone must be succeptible to aerial attack from the enemy during wartime, military strategists concluded. Goethals appealed to the War Department for an air defense system for the Canal, including airplanes and dirigibles to patrol the zone.

On August 9, 1913 President Wilson hastily signed an executive order forbidding flights over the Panama Canal without written consent of the government. Violation of the order carried a fine of $1,000 per infraction and up to one year in prison. Fowler had demonstrated, without even trying, the vulnerability of an enterprise in which so much American money was invested. Fowler found it amusing that such an unpublicized flight would cause such a stir in Washington. One year later he would find it less amusing.

The *Aero Club of America Bulletin* in June, 1913 included a three paragraph announcement that grudgingly credited Fowler with his achievement. The editors, who had published a two-page description of why Hare and Welsh had not attempted the flight in April of the previous year, down-played Fowler's achievement by stating: "That Fowler should have made the flight under practically unchanged conditions does not mean that he was unduly daring. He found what he considered suitable conditions and made the flight. Many things that were supposed impossible a year ago are accomplished to-day: that is progress."

Not only did they fail to mention that the flight was non-stop, but they did not give Fowler credit for his success in making a flight so smooth under such harsh conditions as to allow a motion picture camera to operate for the duration of the flight and create usable footage of the entire flight. This brief mention in the *Aero Club of America Bulletin* of such an important event illustrates the intense competition between aviators of the time and the favoritism for certain aviators among members of the trade press. Fowler was rarely given appropriate credit for his accomplishments because he was not one of the favorites and did not go out of his way to bring attention to himself or his projects. He went about his business quietly and carefully, preparing and planning for each possible contingency. He carried out his tasks responsibly, without unnecessary risk to man or machine. Perhaps this explains Bob Fowler's relative "unknown" status even among aviation historians.

Bob and Ray returned to San Francisco and immediately began work on marketing the valuable motion picture footage of the Canal zone. For a brief period during that summer Bob returned to Kansas City, Missouri where he had operated a flying field the previous summer. He managed that field, flying exhibitions and promoting aviation in general. On August 16, 1913 Bob Fowler and Josephine Conway were married in the courtroom of Justice Casimir Welch. After the ceremony at the courthouse, Fowler drove back to the aviation field and fulfilled an exhibition engagement while his bride awaited his safe return on the ground. Thus began their marriage, which showed signs of strain almost from the beginning. Fowler moved his new family home to San Francisco that fall, and got back to work marketing the Panama pictures. He entered negotiations with *Sunset Magazine* editor Charles K. Field who planned an educational article for the spring of 1914.

Bob created a production in which he displayed the Fowler-Gage biplane on stage, spoke about his trans-isthmian flight and presented the motion pictures. Titled "Panama and the Canal from an Aeroplane," the show was presented in an educational/entertainment format, and Fowler excelled. Fowler and Duhem's motion picture footage was augmented with still photographs by noted photographer Edward Kemp who had documented the entire construction process for more than eight years. The shows were popular and very well attended.

Presentations in theaters throughout San Francisco and Los Angeles brought a great deal of attention to the moving pictures, but when *Sunset Magazine* published its article, the national exposure brought trouble to everyone involved. Fowler was stunned to be arrested at his San Francisco home by deputy U.S. marshals in July of 1914. Also arrested were Ray Duhem,

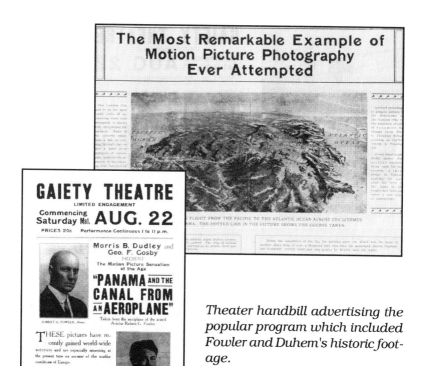

The Most Remarkable Example of Motion Picture Photography Ever Attempted

GAIETY THEATRE
LIMITED ENGAGEMENT

Commencing
Saturday Mat. **AUG. 22**

PRICES 20c   Performance Continuous 1 to 11 p.m.

Morris B. Dudley and
Geo. F. Cosby
PRESENT
The Motion Picture Sensation
of the Age

"PANAMA AND THE CANAL FROM AN AEROPLANE"

Taken from the aeroplane of the noted
Aviator Robert G. Fowler

THESE pictures have recently gained world-wide notoriety and are especially interesting at the present time on account of the warlike conditions of Europe.

Positively the only pictures ever taken of that ever can be taken of Panama and the canal from the air for exhibition as the United States government has forbidden any future flights in the canal zone.

Theater handbill advertising the popular program which included Fowler and Duhem's historic footage.

Charles Field of *Sunset Magazine* and Riley E. Scott, author of the magazine article. The four defendants were charged with violation of a federal statute enacted March 3, 1911 which prohibited divulging photographs, maps or any other military information to any party except the War Department. Penalties were $1,000 per infraction and imprisonment for one year. If such information was passed to a foreign party, the term of imprisonment was increased to ten years. Released on their own recognizance, the four men became celebrities in the San Francisco area. Public sentiment was that the suit was groundless, since permission had been granted by both the War Department and Colonel Goethals prior to the flight. *Sunset's* Field further pointed out that at the time the photographs were taken, only preliminary grading had been completed at most of the future fortification sites. For more than one year, the case dragged on until on June 15, 1915 the Grand Jury issued a statement of Ignoramus, literally " we take no notice." The case was thrown out for lack of evidence.

CANAL PICTURES CAUSE OF ARREST

Government Orders Prosecution of Editor Charles K. Field and Three Others.

DEPARTMENT IS AROUSED

Publication of Photographs of Canal Fortifications Ends in an Unexpected Manner.

CHARLES K. FIELD, editor of Sunset; Aviator Robert Fowler, and Ray Duhem, moving-picture operator, who have been arrested by the Federal authorities for violation of the statute forbidding the photographing of Government fortifications.

PRELIMINARY HEARING TODAY.

DEFENDANTS SURPRISED

SAYS GOETHALS PERMITTED IT.

THE FEDERAL STATUTE.

AUTOISTS GLAD FOR BEACH PARKING PLACES

Action of Park Commissioners Meets With Hearty Approval ---Motor Car Notes.

By LEON J. PINKSON.

DANES GOES TO IDAHO.

FIRESTONE AGENT VISITS CITY.

WHITE TRUCK FOR OIL COMPANY.

Wilson Appointee on His Way to New Post

Malcom A. Franklin of Mississippi Succeeds E. R. Stackable as the Collector of Customs at Hawaii.

Ice Cream Barons in a Legal Tangle

Merchants Ice and Cold Storage Sues National Company and Directors.

Long-Missing Widow Is Said to Be Found

Colorado Lawyer Discovers "Geor...

Stockton Plans to

Local newspapers followed the story. Public sentiment swayed in the direction of Fowler and his group. Courtesy San Francisco Chronicle

IN THE DISTRICT COURT OF THE UNITED STATES, IN AND FOR THE

NORTHERN DISTRICT OF CALIFORNIA,

FIRST DIVISION.

UNITED STATES OF AMERICA,

                    Plaintiff,

          -vs-

CHARLES K. FIELD, RILEY E. SCOTT,
ROBERT G. FOWLER, and RAY A. DUHEM,

                    Defendants.
- -- - - - - - - - - - - - - - - -

I G N O R A M U S .

          The Grand Jurors of the United States of
America, within and for the State and Northern District of
California, do hereby ignore the charge brought against the
defendants above named for a violation of the Act of March
3rd 1911, to wit, taking pictures of the fortifications of
the Panama Canal.

          Dated June 15th 1915.

                              M. M. Concanon
                              _____
                                        Foreman.

CHAPTER NINE

FLIGHT, FAMILY AND FIRSTS
Photos of the Later Years

Robert Fowler's life settled down after the federal case against him was dropped in 1915. The city of San Francisco was preparing to host the Panama-Pacific International Exposition and he accepted an offer to run the "Flying-Boat Concession" at the exposition. He was among those who investigated the fatal crash of Lincoln Beachey in his Taube Monoplane on Sunday, March 14. Famous for "looping the loop," Beachey did not realize that his rate of speed was too great a strain on the wings of the monoplane. The wings were subjected to immense back pressure and did not have bracing wires to take the strain. The wings folded back, transforming the little plane into a missile rocketing toward the ocean.

Fowler estimated that Beachey was traveling at more than 180 miles per hour when he began the fatal dive. Because the experienced aviator was unaccustomed to the protection of an enclosed fuselage, he could not feel the enormous wind pressure. Had he realized his speed, he would have leveled the plane to a gliding angle to reduce the strain. The wings folded at an elevation of 1,000 feet and without any means of control, he could only ride it down. Beachey crashed into the bay at about 300 miles per hour before a crowd of 50,000 spectators. The broken leg and facial abrasions he sustained in the crash would not have been fatal, but he drowned while trying to extricate himself from the safety straps holding him in the seat.

Fowler correctly predicted that stunt flying would cost more lives as aviation grew more popular. The *San Francisco*

Chronicle quoted Fowler: "The science of aviation will be advanced more rapidly by safe and sane methods. French war aviators have covered 1,100,000 miles since the fighting began, with a less percentage of fatalities than during the entire previous year. And they have done so in the worst weather and while dodging bullets. The reason is that they have attempted no circus stunts." Fowler served as an honorary pall bearer at Lincoln Beachey's funeral several days later.

The 1915 Panama-Pacific International Exposition at San Francisco was a world-class event. It drew remarkable crowds and reinforced the city's reputation as the west coast's premier cultural center. Above, the aviation field where Lincoln Beachey took off on his fatal flight. Below, Beachey waves goodbye as he takes off for the last time. Courtesy Donna Ewald Collection.

During a landing on San Francisco Bay, a piece of Fowler's shattered prop flew to shore and sliced into the brim of a derby hat worn by Art Johnson of Dayton, Ohio. Johnson was not injured by the runaway propeller, but ironically died a few days later in an automobile wreck.

Bob Fowler operated the Burgess Flight Training School in 1915 and served as a flight instructor.

Fowler, at left, flew this Burgess-Dunne "Tail-less" Seaplane at Port Washington, Long Island in 1915 while involved with Burgess Company and Curtis. Their motto of "safety first" was Bob's own mantra.

L-W-F ENGINEERING

Robert Fowler co-founded in 1916 the L-W-F Engineering Company in Long Island City, New York. The company name was derived from the initials of the three founders, Ted Lowe, Charles F. Willard and Fowler. Fowler's own patent #1,307,002 for a plywood construction technique gave way to the company's introduction of the first successful monocoque fuselage in an airplane. The result was an aircraft of unusually sleek and streamlined design for its time. But life on the east coast did not agree with the native Californian, and, restless to return home, Bob sold his interest in the business and moved back to the west coast. Charles Willard also left the company. Fowler had stayed with the operation for less that one year.

Interior views from L-W-F Engineering Company. Above, workers pose beside a monocoque fuselage under construction.

FOWLER AIRPLANE CORPORATION

Early in the spring of 1917 Bob began the Fowler Airplane Corporation. U.S. involvment in World War I was a determining factor in the success of this venture. Fowler established a sizable factory on 12th Street near Howard in San Francisco, and in August of 1917 received a coveted government contract to produce war planes. The military standard of the time was the JN4D or "Jenny," a design of the Curtiss Company. Fowler Airplane Corporation records and correspondence reveal the difficulties of fulfilling a government contract while adhering to the design plans of another company. Information was difficult to obtain and design plans were often either inconsistent or incomplete. Fowler and his partners rose to the challenge and by the end of the war had produced 275 Jennies for the Signal Corps.

A devastating fire which spread from an adjacent factory engulfed Fowler's assembly plant on May 21, 1918. Fifteen airplanes in production were destroyed along with a large amount of spruce lumber and linen used for wing covering. The building

Exterior view of Fowler Airplane Corporation's factory and offices on 12th Street at Howard in San Francisco.

lay in ruins. It appears that after the fire Fowler moved his company away from airplane construction to airplane sales and service. The company became the sole western distributor for British-built Avro airplanes, and operated a successful passenger carrying and charter service in the Bay area.

Top and bottom, the interior of Fowler Airplane Corporation.

Interiors of the Fowler Airplane Corporation factory. Below a Jenny nearing completion.

Above, completed Jennies are lined up in a San Francisco field awaiting test flights. Below, a new Jenny takes to the air for the first time as members of Fowler Airplane Corporation look on.

Above, Fowler and partners admire their work. Below, at aviation events Fowler frequently displayed the four cylinder motor from the Wright Model B he flew across the continent.

EXTRA!

TWO CENTS · THE CALL · AFTERNOON EDITION

HUGE S. F. FIRE!

U.S. PLANE FACTORY AFIRE, 100 HOMELESS LOSS ONE MILLION

FLAMES' TOLL AT A GLANCE

750,000 YOUNG MEN FOR ARMY IN JUNE DRAFT, SAYS CROWDER

Scenes from the dramatic fire that destroyed Fowler Airplane Corporation's factory and an adjoining business on May 21, 1918.

Bob flies over San Francisco with a passenger in his "Bluebird" which was available to charter for short hops or longer trips to other cities.

Leonore Vargas in the 1920s, about the time Bob Fowler intro-
duced her to aviation. She would not only become his wife, but
one of the nation's most accomplished female glider pilots.

By the early 1920s Bob's marriage to Josephine had come to an end, and with the closure of Fowler Airplane Corporation came a brief hiatus from aviation. He began work as a sales agent for automobiles in the San Jose and Santa Clara area. His work in the automotive field took him to Chicago for a few years. When his mother's death (his father had passed away several years before) brought him back to California, he met and fell in love with Leonore Vargas, who was also recently divorced and raising her three small children. Leonore, whom Bob nicknamed "Len Bug," "Firefly" or just "Len" was the love of his life. He joined with Len in raising her three children, Marshall J. "Jack," Janet and little Gloria. A strong bond formed between the children and their "Daddy Bob," as they called him. Bob thrived on his newfound family life. Although Leonore and Bob had no children together, Bob raised Leonore's children as his own.

Leonore's first glider flight was a mistake. She was to be towed behind a car-slowly so as to rise only a few feet off the ground-and get a small taste of flying. The driver of the tow car forgot that he was pulling a novice and he took off. So did Leonore, who experimented with the controls and rose to a height of two hundred feet. She was hooked, and became the nation's third female glider pilot.

Leads Field in Duration Flights

10,000 See Lone Glider Pilot in Six-Mile Flight

Mrs. Leonore Fowler Captures Honors in Duration Contests for Men, Women.

San Jose, 10,000 strong, witnessed the city's first glider meet yesterday.

While several thousand viewed the primary and secondary glider contests out on Silver Creek road, seven or eight thousand more waited patiently at the Mead and Orr airport, King and Story roads, to see Philip Longyear pilot his Bowlus sailplane in after a six-mile glide from Grand View home on the Mt. Hamilton road.

Longyear, when he landed, was given something of the aviation transcontinental fliers review. Nearly every person on the field joined the grand rush to crowd hundreds...

Leonore Fowler (second from left) with other aviators including Bobby Trout, far right.

25TH ANNIVERSARY CELEBRATION
PANAMA FLIGHT

On April 27, 1938, Pan American Airways hosted a commemorative flight across the Isthmus of Panama on the 25th anniversary of Bob Fowler's historic flight. Bob, Leonore and several invited guests joined with government officials and dignitaries on board a 21-passenger Douglas transport courtesy of Pan American Airways for the brief flight over the canal zone. The flight's most satisfying moment for Bob must have been looking out the window and seeing three blue and yellow U.S. Army bombers at each wing escorting the transport. As the transport and her escorts winged above Panama City, three PBY Navy patrol bombers from the Fleet Air Base at Coco Solo dropped from the clouds above and formed a V over the Douglas. Fowler was humbled by the attention and praise, and was struck by the contrast between his treatment as a spy in the aftermath of his historic flight and his celebrity status on its 25th anniversary. On his lap during the commemorative flight was a small American flag shellacked to a sheet of glass. Although it was badly deteriorated, its stars and stripes were still plainly visible. It was the same flag which had flown from the wing of the Fowler-Gage on that April morning in 1913 when he and Ray Duhem quietly made history.

Above, Bob boards the Douglas transport plane for the commemorative trip across the Isthmus of Panama. Below, the Douglas transport with Bob and guests aboard is escorted by six U.S. Army bombers over the Panama Canal as three U.S. Navy PBY patrol bombers bring up the rear.

Above, Leonore and Bob join with Paul E. Garber, curator of the Smithsonian Institution National Air Museum in dedicating the Fowler-Gage to the museum's collection. Below, Bob with a section of the Fowler-Gage biplane.

FAMILY DAYS

Bob and Leonore enjoyed traveling by plane well into their golden years, attending aviation events worldwide. Bob was an active member of the Early Birds, the nation's foremost organization of pioneer aviators, and traveled often with Leonore to events throughout the nation.

Above, Bob and Leonore were present in Yuma, Arizona for the dedication of a plaque commemorating Bob's landing there on October 25, 1911. Fowler was the first aviator to land in Yuma and the first to fly across the California/Arizona border.

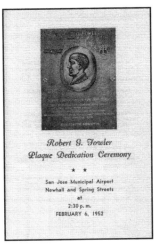

In 1952 a plaque bearing his likeness was dedicated at the San Jose Municipal Airport (now the San Jose International Airport) in honor of his achievements as a pioneer aviator.

Bob corrects Robert Ripley of "Ripley's Believe it or Not" after Ripley's column incorrectly credited a pilot by the name of Wynn with the first non stop ocean to ocean flight in 1917.

Bob at his desk at home. An avid correspondent, he stayed in touch with friends from his early days in aviation, wrote articles for aviation journals and founded the Pacific Aero Club.

Bob receives his certificate as a life member of the Silver Wings Organization.

Bob displays the engine of the Wright Model B at an aviation event in the 1960s. He proudly wears the checkered cap of the Early Birds.

Above, dedication of a plaque in 1940 honoring early fliers who were trained by the Wright brothers at Huffman Prairie. Bob Fowler is third from left and Orville Wright is third from right. Below, the plaque showing Robert G. Fowler as the first west to east coast aviator.

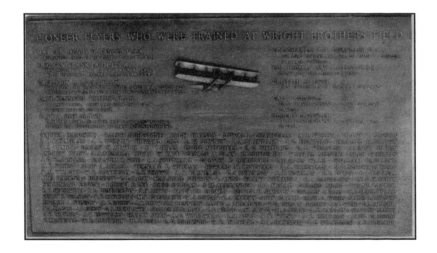

Above, Bob in an early Curtiss Pusher. Below, *in a 1930s era glider. In addition to his contributions to the field of powered flight, he was active with Leonore in glider flying, and was a member of the Quiet Birdmen.*

Above, Bob goes up for a flight in an F104 jet at Hampton Air Force Base in the 1960s. His lifelong dedication to aviation spanned the incredible distance between the first flight of the Wright brothers to the era of jet propulsion, from a three-month journey from coast to coast to a six hour hop from New York to Los Angeles. Below, he visits with a young fan at the San Jose Airport at the premier of the popular 1960s motion picture "Those Magnificent Men in their Flying Machines."

Above, Bob visits with old friend and early Wright pilot Frank T. Coffyn. They often enjoyed comparing flying experiences in the early Wrights. Coffyn was a co-member of many of the same aviation organizations and the two spent many hours reminiscing in later years. Old friends in aviation were few because of the inherent danger of early flying. Many of Fowler's earliest aviation friends, Lincoln Beachey, Eugene Ely, Arch Hoxsey, John B. Moisant and many others were dead by the 1920s. Below, Bob and Len look at an early photo of Bob in his flying gear.

Bob waves from the cockpit of a World War I-era "Jenny."

Into the final years of his life, Bob participated in aviation groups such as the Pacific Aero Club, Early Birds, Quiet Birdmen, National Aeronautics Association, Silver Wings, American Aviation Historical Society, OX-5 Club, Western Glider Association, San Jose Flying Club and others. He continued to promote aviation as an industry and lobby for additional airports nationwide.

Robert G. Fowler lost his wife Leonore on March 10, 1965. His health, which had declined in the previous year continued to erode after her death, and on June 15, 1966 he passed away at the age of 82. Bob died quietly in his San Jose home, an old man who had lived a fulfilling life, long enough even to teach his his grandchildren to drive. The fact that he did not die at the controls of an early airplane in a blaze of glory may have disqualified him for elite status as one of aviation's best-known pioneers. Robert G. Fowler's contributions to early aviation cannot be counted by a simple tally of daredevil stunts and broken records. This careful, courageous, inventive man was one of America's most prolific pioneers who believed firmly in the future of aviation and lived his life to that end.

AVIATION'S PIONEERS

OX5 CLUB OF AMERICA ... AVIATION HALL OF FAME

> Dedicated to the Men and Women who risked Life and Fortune to establish the Great Aviation Industry. They were Beacons of Light in the Embryonic Age of Flight.

THIS IS TO CERTIFY THAT

Robert G. Fowler

HAS BEEN SELECTED AS A MEMBER OF THE

OX5 CLUB OF AMERICA
AVIATION HALL OF FAME

AND IS AWARDED THIS HONOR IN RECOGNITION OF CONTRIBUTIONS TO THE ESTABLISHMENT OF THE AIR INDUSTRY.

By authority of Board of Governors and the undersigned officers of the OX5 CLUB of AMERICA, THIS 6TH DAY OF OCTOBER 1973.

By *W. Buril Barclay*
                    PRESIDENT

Harold Voelter
                    SECRETARY

NEWSPAPERS, MAGAZINES

Aero Club of America Bulletin-April 1912, June 1913
Aero Digest-September 1946
Bainbridge Search Light-Bainbridge, Georgia, February 1912
Beaumont Journal-December, 1911
Colfax Record-September 1911, February 1912
Daily Herald-Gulfport and Biloxi Mississippi, January 1912
The Daily Picayune-New Orleans-Dec.1911-Jan. 1912
Democrat-Star-Pascagoula, Mississippi, January 1912
Dothan Eagle-Dothan, Alabama-January
Flying Pioneers Biographies of Harold E. Morehouse
Fort Worth Record-November 1911
Grass Valley Union-September 1911
Handwritten Flight Log-Robert G. Fowler, 1911-1912
Handwritten Panama Diary-Robert G. Fowler, 1913
Houston Chronicle-December 1911
Lake Charles Daily Times-December 1911
Los Angeles Examiner-October 1911
Mobile Register-January 1912
Nevada County Historical Society Newsletter-April 1976
New York Times-September 1911-February 1912
Oakland Tribune-September 1911
Pasadena Daily News-October 1911
Riverside Daily Press-October 1911
Sacramento Union-September 1911
San Francisco Call and Post-July 11, 1914
San Francisco Chronicle-September 1911, March 1915
San Jose Mercury News-1928, 1929, 1936, 1948, 1960-66
Sweetwater Weekly Reporter-Sweetwater, TX-November 1911
Troy Messenger-Troy, Alabama-January-February 1912

BIBLIOGRAPHY

Bohrer, Walt and Ann. *Twenty Smiling Eagles*: Vantage Press, Inc. 1962

Ewald, Donna and Clute, Peter. *San Francisco Invites the World*: Chronicle Books. 1991

Marrero, Frank. *Lincoln Beachey The Man Who Owned the Sky:* Scottwall Associates. 1997

Stein, E.P. *Flight of the Vin Fiz:* Arbor House Publishing Company. 1985

Wright, Orville. *How We Invented the Airplane An Illustrated History*: Dover Publications. 1953, 1988

Photographic Sources

Donna Ewald Photographic Collection
Ed and Charlene Fontana
Fowler Family Archives
John P. Ingle, Jr.
Nevada County Historical Society Newsletter
San Diego Aerospace Museum
San Jose Mercury News
Schwab, Ellard and Buzz
Searls Historical Library, Nevada City, California
Wright State University Photographic Archives

Photographs and documents without credit in the caption are from the Fowler Family Archives, Carol Osborne, Archivist.

INDEX

INDEX

Index

INDEX

INDEX